The Computer : Yours Obediently

Now Use the Computer

Teachers' Book 3a

Basic

Scottish Computers in Schools Project

W & R Chambers Edinburgh

Illustrations : Tim Smith

© Scottish Computers in Schools Project

First published 1975

ISBN 0 550 77113 1

Printed in Great Britain by
Newgate Press Ltd
London EC1

Scottish Computers in Schools Project

Director   **N M Smart**   Aberdeen College of Education

Members   **A W McMeeken**   Dundee College of Education
J M Rushforth   University of Dundee
D U Steele   Aberdeen College of Education

General Preface

Some recent educational reports, for example Curriculum Papers 6 and 11 'Computers and the Schools' (Scottish Education Department, 1969 and 1972) and 'Computer Education for All' (The Mathematical Association, 1969), have drawn attention to the growing influence of the computer in modern society and the consequent need to acquaint the majority of pupils with the uses—and limitations—of the computer in solving the everyday problems of industry, business, government, etc. Common to these reports is the recommendation that an introductory course on computer studies should form part of the general education of most pupils, and that such courses should be given by non-mathematics as well as mathematics teachers.

To meet this need the members of the Scottish Computers in Schools Project have designed an elementary course on computer studies entitled *The Computer: Yours Obediently*. Catering for a wide range of ability, it can be started with pupils at the age range 13-14 or at any later stage which the teacher finds convenient. The series of books for the course consists of pupils' books with corresponding pupils' workbooks, and teachers' books. The workbooks ensure plenty of pupil activity in the teaching of the course.

The teachers' books serve two purposes. Firstly, they provide a self-contained introduction to the subject of 'computing' for teachers, especially those who have little or no mathematical or scientific background; and secondly, by means of suitable references to the pupils' texts, they act as supplementary teaching material to be used in conjunction with the pupils' material. In the case of the programming books of Part Three, extra examples are suggested.

Each of the teachers' packs (consisting of teachers' books to accompany a particular pupils' text) incorporates a set of slides for use in the teaching situation.

Part Three of the Project contains neither pupils' workbooks nor slides.

Answers to the exercises in Book 3a (BASIC) are provided at the end of this book.

Preface to Teachers' Book 3a

The object of Book 3a on BASIC is to introduce the various elementary concepts of computer programming one at a time. Each chapter deals with a separate idea so that this can be assimilated before any further advance is made. The main features dealt with are:

(i) assignment statements—allowing straightforward manipulations of formulae (Chapter 3)
(ii) input and output—allowing, for instance, printing of text and simple lay-out of results (Chapter 4)
(iii) loops—demonstrating the ability of the computer to perform repetitive tasks (Chapter 5)
(iv) lists—using subscripted variables in a one-dimensional array (Chapter 6)
(v) jumps—showing how decisions can be taken and how the order in which instructions are executed can be altered (Chapter 7).

In each of these chapters the examples and exercises are as simple as possible so that the student learns the technique being described without becoming too involved in extraneous logical processes.

In the remaining chapters we write more advanced programs which include both loops and jumps and we show how one loop may be put inside another. Finally we introduce the idea of a table, which is an extension of the concept of a list and consists of elements which possess two subscripts.

Whilst the latter chapters do not introduce new kinds of program statements, they do involve deeper logical thinking and may prove more difficult for some students. It is hoped, however, that they will be of value to those whose interest has been aroused and who wish to do more complex work.

In preparing this Teachers' Book we have borne in mind the teacher who may be teaching programming for the first time or, indeed, who may have to teach himself programming with its aid. We would suggest that such a person should do some practical programming before attempting to teach it. This means that he must actually write programs and have them run at the centre which he is to use. By doing this practical work he will learn not only the language but also the commands needed to get a program run on the computer and he will become familiar with the error messages which come back to him if he makes mistakes. As a beginner he will inevitably make mistakes but this can be beneficial to him since he will later spend a proportion of his time correcting similar mistakes made by students.

He will quickly realise that he has to obey the syntax of the language before his program can run. Also, he must always check that his program gives the right answers, since a wrong answer is worse than none at all. In this respect, he is advised to use simple numerical data for testing, since this makes manual checking of the result much easier.

For the reader with no previous programming experience we would suggest that he teaches himself the fundamentals by working through the first seven chapters of Book 3a.

The reader who has already had experience in programming in FORTRAN or ALGOL should have no difficulty in writing in BASIC. As the language is simpler than either of these, he need only familiarise himself with the forms of the program statements.

Each chapter of the Teachers' Book (except Chapters 10 and 11) corresponds to a chapter in Book 3a. Commentary on the subject of each chapter is followed, where appropriate, by additional material and exercises. Solutions to all of the exercises are at the end of the book.

One of the best incentives for learning programming is the need to use it for problem solving and, whilst we have provided examples and exercises for practice, students should be allowed to write programs to solve their own problems when these occur, provided that they are within each student's capacity.

Contents

General preface
Preface to Teachers' Book 3a

I **Introducing the computer** 11

II **A simple program**
1 An example 13
2 Line numbering 14
3 The REM statement 14
4 The END statement 15
5 Additional exercises 15

III **Doing arithmetic**
1 Introduction 16
2 The use of symbols 16
3 Arithmetic operators 16
4 Evaluation of arithmetic expressions 17
5 The form of arithmetic expressions 17
6 Brackets 18
7 Standard functions 19
8 Line numbering 19
9 Testing and checking programs 19
10 Improvements to programming techniques 20
11 More standard functions 21
12 Error messages 22
13 Additional exercises 23

IV **Input and output**
1 READ and INPUT statements 26
2 Printing of numbers and text 26
3 Implementation of the READ statements 27
4 Arithmetic expressions in PRINT statements 28
5 A particular use for the READ statement 28
6 Additional exercises 29

V Loops
1 Introduction 30
2 The use of loops for repetitive operations 30
3 The FOR statement and the counting variable 30
4 Using a variable as a limit in the FOR statement 31
5 Using the counting variable in the loop 32
6 Additional exercises 32

VI Lists
1 Introduction 34
2 Elementary manipulation of list elements 34
3 Use of a variable as a subscript 34
4 Loops and lists 35
5 Subscript checking 36
6 Additional exercises 36

VII Jumps
1 Introduction 37
2 The computer's power to discriminate 37
3 Flow charts involving decisions 38
4 Notation for comparison symbols 39
5 More general relations 39
6 Floating point arithmetic 40
7 Additional exercises 41

VIII More jumps and loops
1 Introduction 42
2 Exit from a loop 42
3 More than one decision box 47
4 Multiple decisions 50
5 Using jumps in FOR statements 50
6 A further example 51
7 Change of step length 52
8 Counting in non-integer steps 53
9 Loops inside loops 53
10 Additional exercises 55

IX   Problem solving using lists and tables
1   Retaining information in lists   57
2   Lists of varying lengths   57
3   The problem of finding the largest number in a list   58
4   The problem of comparing lists   58
5   Tables   59
6   Drawing a histogram   61
7   Additional exercises   63

X   Additional facilities in BASIC
1   Introduction   65
2   The ON statement   65
3   The RESTORE facility   66
4   The TAB function   67
5   User-defined functions   69
6   Subroutines   70
7   The history of BASIC   72
8   A standard BASIC   72
9   Additional exercises   72

XI   An interactive example
1   Introduction   74
2   Definition of the problem   74
3   Representation of the board in the computer   76
4   Making moves   76
5   A subroutine to find the position on the board   77
6   A subroutine for throwing the die   78
7   A flow chart to describe the game   78
8   The main program   81
9   Additional exercises   82

Solutions to exercises in Book 3a and Teachers' Book 3a   82

1 Introducing the computer

Since many students will already have learned something about computers before starting on a programming book, this chapter is simply a quick reminder about the general background to computers.

It may be too brief for students being introduced to computers for the first time, in which case the teacher will want to spend a little time in describing computers and how they function. These topics are discussed in detail in *Introducing the Computer*, Teachers' Book 1a of *The Computer: Yours Obediently*. Together with a selection of the slides from Teachers' Pack 1, it is possible to give these students sufficient background information for them to understand what happens in a computer room and what programming is about.

It is not necessary for students to know anything about the internal workings of a computer before they can start program-writing.

They should be clear about a program being a set of instructions to the computer, about the concept of a stored program and about the difference between a program and the data used by a program. They should also know that both program and data have to be converted into a machine-readable form, e.g. on to punched cards, and that their BASIC program statements need to be translated by the computer into a lower-level machine language before they can be run. The concept of the storage and retrieval of information is vital, since the whole of program-writing depends on putting data into named locations and retrieving this data for subsequent manipulation.

The degree of emphasis given to operating systems and interactive computing depends on how the work of the class is processed. It is probably best to deal with the particular system in use. The teacher can demonstrate with both input and output from work that has been run on his local machine.

At this point it may be desirable to discuss the program in Chapter 2 of Book 3a and, when this has been done, to show the stages it passes through in being processed.

If a visit can be arranged to the computer installation which handles the students' work, this gives them an opportunity to see the whole process in operation. It can be a valuable experience for many of them. For such a visit to be useful, however, an adequate introduction should first be provided in class.

In Book 3a we have avoided two points relating to the 'translation' of BASIC into a lower-level language. In the first place, we do not say how this translation occurs. On some computers a program called a *compiler* is used to achieve this, on others a different technique using an *interpreter* is employed. In both cases the BASIC program statements are stored in the computer, thus allowing them to be altered later if required.

With a compiler, all the BASIC statements are converted into the lower-level machine at the beginning. The program is then said to be *compiled* and a further instruction can be given which causes the program to be run.

With an interpreter, the BASIC statements are interpreted into the low-level language and executed one by one, so that whilst the program is running the process of interpreting instructions is going on.

There will be no obvious difference to the user whichever method is being employed except possibly when grammatical errors are made in the BASIC statements.

The second point concerns errors in BASIC statements. We avoid mentioning this topic in Book 3a until the end of Chapter 3, since it seems better to let the student start writing programs before telling him of all the mistakes he might make.

2 A simple program

1 An example

We believe that students should try writing programs as early in their course as is practicable. Hence we introduce programming by demonstrating with a very simple flow chart and its accompanying program.

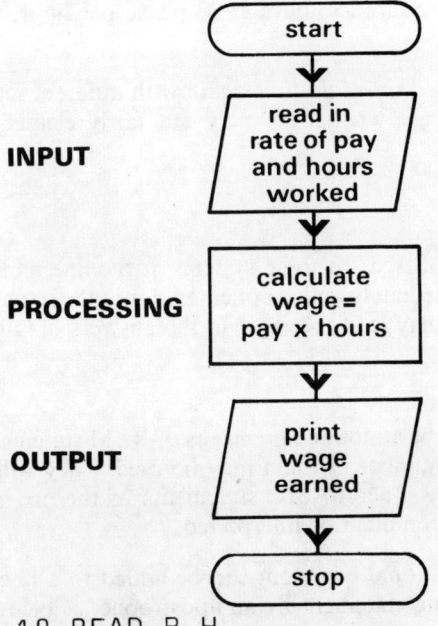

```
10 READ R,H
20 LET W = R*H
30 PRINT W
40 DATA 50,12
50 REM THE PROGRAM NOW CONCLUDES
60 REM WITH AN END STATEMENT
70 END
```

We have assumed a very elementary knowledge of flow charts, merely using rectangular boxes for processing statements, parallelograms for input and output statements and boxes with rounded ends for the 'start' and 'stop' symbols.

If further teaching is required on drawing flow charts there are a number of elementary examples (not related to computing) in Book 2 of the series, *Man Uses the Computer*, and the corresponding Teachers' Book 2a, *Mind Over Matter*.

The students should be able to see that the specimen program above merely calculates the product of two numbers and prints the result.

At this stage it is sufficient to suggest that programs can be written by putting down statements similar to those in the sample program. Emphasis should be laid on the need for exactness in using the grammar correctly, for example in putting commas between items in a READ statement.

The program also demonstrates that we put numbers into boxes (locations) and then manipulate them by writing simple bits of arithmetic, often putting the result into a further box, as in line 20.

The need for line numbering should also be mentioned since the program is executed in ascending order of line number.

It should be pointed out that the program when written works equally well for other items of data and that by changing the DATA statement only we can calculate other results such as 12 hours at 20 pence per hour, 15 hours at 33 pence per hour, 14·5 hours at 16 pence per hour, and so on.

The fact that the same program can be used time and time again with different sets of data is often the reason why programs are written to carry out fairly elementary calculations.

2 Line numbering

It is essential that all lines should be numbered. In some systems, if the line number is omitted, the instruction is executed immediately and is not entered into the sequence of program instructions. This obviously may lead to errors in the answers obtained.

3 The REM statement

As indicated in Book 3a, the program can be annotated by means of REM statements. These may be put in anywhere and any number of them may be used. They will be stored in the computer along with all the other BASIC statements of the program but will be ignored when the program is compiled or interpreted.

In some implementations of BASIC, additional comment can be added to a line by separating the comment from the preceding statement by an apostrophe, as below:

```
50 LET A = 1 ' IS AN EXAMPLE
```
This would be treated as the statement

```
50 LET A = 1
```

If the apostrophe facility is available, it is in fact permissible to write:

```
60 ' THIS WILL DO FOR A REM STATEMENT
```

4 The END statement

We use the END statement as a terminator for our programs. There is also a STOP command. The latter indicates the logical end of the program, which is not necessarily the last instruction. In fact, where a program branches, more than one STOP command may be present. We can easily avoid this rather more complicated structure by arranging, after completing the calculation, to jump to the END statement.

5 Additional exercises

1. Write a program to read the cost of an article followed by the number purchased, and to print out the total cost. (Keep everything in pence.)
2. A lorry known to weigh T tonnes is weighed together with its load. The total weight is W tonnes. Write a program to calculate the weight of the load.
3. Write a program to add together three items of data A,B,C and to print out the three values read in, followed by the sum. (The program should be run a number of times with different data values, e.g. 3, 4, 5; 3,−4,5; 1·2, 2·3, 3·4, etc.)

3 Doing arithmetic

1 Introduction

In this chapter we concentrate on the assignment statement and in particular on the evaluation of arithmetic expressions.

2 The use of symbols

The first problem which the student has to master is the use of symbols, since he is going to be faced with statements such as

```
20 LET W = R*H
```

In any particular run of a program, R and H may have different values and it is because of this that the program can be used repeatedly for different calculations.

The statement can be put into words thus:

> Take the number contained in the box labelled R, multiply it by the number contained in the box labelled H and put the result into the box labelled W.

Strictly we should say 'Take a *copy* of the number contained . . . multiply it by a *copy* of the number . . .', since we would make the point that R and H still contain the same values after the assignment statement has been executed as before it.

3 Arithmetic operators

We introduce the four arithmetic operators, $+$, $-$, $*$, $/$ and build up simple arithmetic expressions from them. Later we introduce the $\uparrow$ symbol, denoting raising to a power. (If students have not encountered squares and cubes this could be omitted.)

Variables can in fact be used on both sides of the $\uparrow$ symbol. We can write

```
10 LET C = A↑B
```

but errors will be indicated if an attempt is made to raise zero to a negative power

16

(e.g. A=0, B=−1) or a negative arithmetic value is raised to a fractional power (e.g. A=−2, B=0·5).

If we are required to evaluate, say, A^{-3} we have to write A↑(−3), since it is not permissible to have two arithmetic operators next to each other.

4 Evaluation of arithmetic expressions

We show in Book 3a how the expression b^2+c^2, where b=2 and c=3, is evaluated by *first* calculating the squares of b and c and *then* by adding the two resulting values. This leads to the suggestion that, during the evaluation of an arithmetic expression, the arithmetic operators are accorded different priorities.

The appropriate table of priorities is:

Operation	Order of priority
↑	1
* and /	2
+ and −	3

In the expression A↑2+5*A −7, with A=3 (Example 4, page 25, in Book 3a), the partial expression A↑2 is evaluated first and this value (9) is temporarily retained in the computer. The expression 5*A(=15) is then calculated and retained. Finally, the additions and subtractions are done and the three values, 9, 15 and 7 are combined into the final result.

It is difficult to say how much emphasis should be laid on teaching the formal evaluation of expressions. The rules are exactly those of elementary algebra and it may be natural for the student to evaluate expressions in the proper way. The only difficulty likely to arise is in statements with a number of multiplications and divisions, e.g. A*B/C*D.

The computer tackles this by first calculating A*B, then dividing this result by C and finally by multiplying the whole by D, which is not the same as $\frac{A*B}{C*D}$. [This last expression has to be written either with brackets, as A*B/(C*D), or as A*B/C/D.]

The most important point to put over is that the computer takes the expression and computes it systematically until eventually it arrives at a single numerical value, which can then be assigned to the variable on the left-hand side of a LET statement.

5 The form of arithmetic expressions

We have avoided the use of the word *variable* in Book 3a since it is a word with which the students may not be familiar. It is, however, a convenient word to describe the name of a location and it is also appropriate since the value in the location can vary during the execution of the program. We will use it in this text where desirable.

The reader may have noticed that all arithmetic expressions take the same form, viz.:

> *variable operator variable operator variable* . . .

$$A \quad + \quad B \quad * \quad C$$

A constant can replace a variable so that we can write:

$$A \quad + \quad 2 \quad * \quad C$$

A single variable or a constant are degenerate forms of an arithmetic expression, which means that assignment statements take the form

      10 LET A=arithmetic expression

where of course the line number and the variable A can be changed. Typical assignment statements are:

```
10 LET A = B+C
20 LET D = 2*E
30 LET P = 3.142
40 LET S = T
```

Other statements, which may look a little peculiar but which are correct and of considerable value, are:

```
10 LET N = N+1
20 LET S = S+A
```

(We do not mention these in Chapter 3 of Book 3a, but introduce them later.)

The first allows a count to be kept in a location N, since it says, 'take the value in N, add 1 to it and put this new value back into N.' The second allows a running total to be obtained, since each time the statement is executed a value A is added to S.

The value of statements such as these becomes evident when we introduce loops.

6 Brackets

In section 8 (page 26 of Book 3a), we introduce brackets with arithmetic expressions to allow evaluations contrary to the natural priority system, i.e. to allow us to calculate A*B/(C*D). When the computer meets an opening bracket it suspends the calculation it was doing and starts evaluating the contents of the bracket. Thus 'things inside the brackets are worked out first'.

The 'thing' inside the bracket is itself an arithmetic expression which can contain further brackets. Thus we can write, for example,

```
((A*B+C)*D-2)*E+6.3
```

Our general plan of an arithmetic expression

> *variable operator variable operator variable* . . .

can now be extended by replacing *variable* by *bracketed arithmetic expression*.

The form of an arithmetic expression explains why all arithmetic operators have to be inserted and why such expressions as 2B, (A+B)C are not permissible. Extra brackets can of course be added for clarity, as in (A*B)/(C*D).

We have commented on the structure of arithmetic expressions for the interest of the teacher. We would on no account suggest that anything more be put over to the student than the suggestion that in a statement such as

```
10 LET Z = A*B+C*D-E
```

the names of locations and the operators alternate.

7 Standard functions

Section 10 (page 28 of Book 3a) deals with the square root function and introduces one of the *standard functions* available in the language. (We mention the others on page 21 of this book.) If the students have met square roots, it is worth while showing that the computer is already programmed in BASIC to calculate these. The function SQR(...) is used like a variable and the content of the brackets is an arithmetic expression. The brackets themselves are obligatory.

8 Line numbering

We refer to the reason for line numbering in tens and to the opportunity it provides for editing a written program. We then discuss the types of errors which can occur in a program. Practical examples of these, relating to messages output by the local system, will be useful here as illustrations.

9 Testing and checking programs

Our final comment on the need to check a program by running it with test data should be emphasised. The students should practise going through a set of statements and doing the necessary evaluations line by line. This technique is often needed when wrong answers are being obtained and the logic of the program statements is suspect.

An example of evaluation is given in Section 9 (page 27 of Book 3a), namely

	A	B	C	D
10 READ A,B	2	3	?	?
20 LET C = A+B	2	3	5	?
30 LET D = A-B	2	3	5	-1
40 LET C = A+B+1	2	3	6	-1
50 LET C = -D	2	3	1	-1
60 LET D = A/(B+C)	2	3	1	0.5
70 PRINT A,B,C,D	2	3	1	0.5
80 DATA 2,3				
90 END				

where we simulate the store and keep a record of the contents of the locations A, B, C and D at the completion of each statement of the program.

Notice in this example that the values of the variables are not known until values have been given to them either by READ statements or by assignment statements.

Many BASIC systems automatically put the value of all the variables to zero at the beginning of a program. However, we do not assume that this is the case and would not recommend taking such a fact for granted. Indeed, if repeated runs of a program are made, the variable may only be set to zero automatically on the first occasion with consequent errors occurring in later runs. We suggest that variables are set to zero by assignment statements such as

```
10 LET A = 0
```

10 Improvements to programming techniques

Since Book 3a is intended for beginners we have not attempted to introduce any elegance into our programming techniques and we would be satisfied if students were to succeed in getting programs working, even if they appeared heavy-handed to an experienced programmer. It might be possible, however, to suggest to brighter students that some improvements may be made.

One such improvement can be made when we want to evaluate a number of expressions, each containing a common sub-expression. For example, if we want to calculate $A+B$, $(A+B)^2$, $(A+B)^3$, and $(A+B)^4$ we *could* write

```
10 READ A,B
20 LET R1 = A+B
30 LET R2 = (A+B)↑2
40 LET R3 = (A+B)↑3
50 LET R4 = (A+B)↑4
60 PRINT R1,R2,R3,R4
70 DATA <TWO DATA VALUES>
80 END
```

but this involves the computer in a lot of unnecessary work. It has to calculate $A+B$ four times and enter routines to square, cube and quadruple the value.

It is more efficient to write

```
10 READ A,B
20 LET R1 = A+B
30 LET R2 = R1*R1
40 LET R3 = R2*R1
50 LET R4 = R3*R1
60 PRINT R1,R2,R3,R4
70 DATA <TWO DATA VALUES>
80 END
```

using the result of R1 to obtain R2, R2 to get R3, and so on.

In computer time, addition and subtraction are faster than multiplication, which in turn is faster than division. The routines to raise to a power or to evaluate any of the standard functions take even longer. It is therefore better to write:

A*A in place of A↑2
1/A in place of A↑(−1)
0·5*A in place of A/2
and even A+A in place of 2*A

However, there comes a point where legibility and understanding are more important than computer time. Only in programs where expressions have to be evaluated many thousands of times do the above considerations make a noticeable difference in the time a job takes on the computer.

11 More standard functions

Besides the square root function introduced in Book 3a there are a number of other functions which can be used in BASIC in the same way. Some of these are strictly mathematical and their use will be obvious to readers likely to require them. These functions are:

> SIN(X), COS(X), TAN(X)—where X is measured in radians
> ATAN(X)—arctan with the value given between $\pm \frac{1}{2}\pi$
> LOG(X), EXP(X)—the natural logarithm and the exponential function

The argument X in these or any other standard functions can be a constant, a variable, an arithmetic expression or indeed another standard function. We could, for instance, write

```
10 LET A = SQR(B*B+C*C-2*B*C*COS(A1*3.142/180))
```

which is the cosine formula for the length of the side *a* of the triangle ABC whose angle A is contained in A1 and has been measured in *degrees*.

Four other standard functions, which are of wider application, are also available.

The function ABS(X) provides the facility for obtaining the magnitude (absolute value) of a number irrespective of its sign. If, for instance, we wanted to obtain the *magnitude* of the difference between two numbers A and B, we could write:

```
10 LET M = ABS(A-B)
```

If A=7, B=3, the value in M would be 4.
If A=2, B=8, the value in M would be 6.

The statement

```
20 LET Z = SQR(ABS(W))
```

would ensure that a square root would be obtained even if the number in W were negative.

If we wished to test two numbers A and B to see if they differed by less than, say, 0·0001 we might write:

```
10 IF A-B<0.0001
```

This is *not* sufficient however, since, if B is greater than A, the left-hand side of this inequality is negative and therefore less than 0·0001.

We must say:

```
10 IF ABS(A-B)<0.0001
```

This ensures that the difference between A and B lies between $\pm$0·0001.

The ABS function is frequently employed in tests of this nature but, since it involves the use of the IF statement, we defer any further reference until the conclusion of Chapter 7 on page 41.

The function SGN(X) examines the sign of X and gives the value 1 if X is positive, zero if X is zero and -1 if X is negative.

The function INT(X) is used to obtain the integer part of a number, so that INT(3·7)=3 and INT(2·1)=2. More strictly, INT(X) is defined as the largest integer *less than or equal to* X. Thus, if X is itself an integer, INT(X)=X. If X is negative and not an integer, then INT(X) will be *less* than X. For example, INT(-1·2)= -2 (*not* -1).

If we wish to find the integer nearest to a given number we write INT(X+0·5). Take, for example, the case where X=3·3. Then INT(X+0·5)=INT(3·8)=3, which is correct since 3 is the nearest integer to 3·3. If, however, X=3·7 then INT(X+0·5)= INT(4·2)=4, and the nearest integer to 3·7 is 4.

The INT function is useful when we require to know the quotient and remainder after carrying out division. For instance, if we wish to convert 5327 pence to pounds and pence we divide by 100 to obtain 53·27. The function INT(53·27) gives the number of pounds and the pence are obtained by subtracting 53×100 from the original value.

A program to do the conversion is:

```
10 READ P
20 LET L = INT(P/100)
30 LET P = P-L*100
40 PRINT L,P
50 DATA<VALUE IN PENCE>
60 END
```

The random number generator RND(X) produces a value lying between 0 and 1. Repeated use produces similar values, the set of values satisfying statistical tests for randomness.

We can obtain other ranges for the random number by multiplication and, together with the INT facility, we can get a random distribution of integers. The following statement*, for example, produces numbers corresponding to the throw of a die.

```
510 LET V = INT(6*RND(A)+1)
```

The argument X of the RND does not have to be assigned each time it is used. Depending on the computer, it may be possible to give an initial value to X to trigger off the random number generator. After that, the value obtained is no longer under the control of the programmer (otherwise the concept of 'randomness' would be violated). The function must, however, be written with a dummy argument for the computer to recognise it.

12 Error messages

We end Chapter 3 with some information on the types of errors which occur in programming and the kind of messages output by the computer but, without going into great detail, it is impossible to elaborate on this subject.

We would earnestly recommend that a teacher should learn by experience and should practise programming in a practical way by submitting jobs to a computer. He thus

* *This statement is used in the example on snakes and ladders in Chapter 11 (page 78).*

22

learns by his errors and in smoothing out his own difficulties he will go a long way to being able to deal with his students' problems later.

13 Additional exercises

1. Write assignment statements to do the following:
     (a) Add P, Q and R and store the result in A.
     (b) Put twice the value contained in A into B.
     (c) Add three times A to twice B and store the result in C.
     (d) Multiply X by Y, add 5 to the result and store in Z.
     (e) Calculate the sum of P and Q and store the result again in P.
2. Write assignment statements to do the following (brackets are required):
     (a) Divide A by the sum of B and C and put the result in D.
     (b) Store the average value of X, Y, Z and W in M.
     (c) Add the contents of B and C and then double this, adding 6 to the result before storing in A.
3. Find the values of A,B,C,D after the execution of each statement in the following programs:
     (a)

```
10 READ A,B
20 LET C = A-B
30 LET D = C-2*A
40 LET C = D-A
50 LET B = C*2
60 LET A = C/2
70 DATA 2,1
80 END
```

     (b)

```
10 READ A,B
20 LET C = A/B
30 LET D = A*A
40 LET C = 1/(A+B)
50 LET C = C+1
60 LET D = (2*A+B)*2+C
70 DATA 1,2
80 END
```

     (c)

```
10 READ C
20 LET A = 1
30 LET B = 1/(A+C)
40 LET D = 1/B
50 LET C = 0
60 LET D = C/D
70 DATA 2
80 END
```

(d)

```
10 READ A,B
20 LET C = A+B
30 LET D = SQR(A↑2+B↑2)
40 DATA 3,4
50 END
```

4. A shopkeeper sells lemonade at 9p per bottle and pays 3p for each empty bottle returned. Write a program to calculate how much money he has made when he has sold M full bottles and received N empties, values for M and N being supplied as data.

5. A motorist is allowed expenses of 4p per kilometre. Write a program which reads in as data the number of kilometres on the clock at the end and at the start of a journey and calculates the expenses for the journey.

6. A salesman sells three types of watches. He sells the first type for £20 and makes a 20% profit, the second type for £8·50 and makes a 10% profit and the third type for £5 and makes an 8% profit. If he sells A watches of the first type, B watches of the second type and C watches of the third type, write a program to calculate the total profit he has made on each type of watch he has sold and his overall profit on all his sales.

7. A circle of radius R has its centre at the centre of a square of side 2R. Write a program which calculates the area between the circle and the square. The length R is to be read as data.

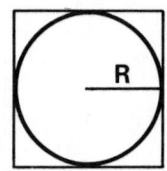

8. A crate of apples costs £1·70, a crate of oranges costs £1·40 and a crate of grapefruit costs £1·80. A hotelier buys M crates of apples, N crates of oranges and P crates of grapefruit. Write a program which reads M, N and P as data and calculates how much his purchases cost.

9. Write a program using the RND function to simulate the throw of two dice and to compute their total.

10. Write a program using the ABS function to calculate (1) the sum of the absolute values of five numbers read as data (2) the absolute value of the sum of the five numbers.

11. Rewrite the following sets of program statements so that they will run more efficiently on the computer.

(a)

```
10 LET W = A+B
20 LET X = 1/(A+B)
30 LET Y = (A+B)/(1+A+B)
40 LET Z = A+B/(1+A+B)
```

24

(b)
```
10 LET P = SQR(A)+SQR(B)
20 LET Q = SQR(A)*SQR(B)
30 LET R = 1+SQR(A)*SQR(B)
```

(c)
```
10 LET P1 = 1/H1/(1/H1+1+1/H2)
20 LET P2 = 1/(1/H1+1+1/H2)
30 LET P3 = 1/H2(1/H1+1+1/H2)
```

4 Input and output

1 READ and INPUT statements

There are two input statements in BASIC, namely READ and INPUT. The former usually requires a DATA statement to complement it (*note:* the IBM 1130 does not use DATA statements) and the latter requires input of data when the program is running.

In some systems, INPUT is limited to interactive use and cannot be used for batch processing. We have therefore chosen to use READ as the input statement and to put our data for the problem into DATA statements. This is inconvenient in that new DATA cards have to be inserted into the program when new data is being evaluated. If the INPUT statement *is* available for batch use, then multiple runs of the program can be carried out by supplying different sets of data at run-time. The teacher should consult his local computer centre for advice and then choose the method best suited to his needs.

It is unnecessary to elaborate on what is in Book 3a on READ and DATA statements except to remark that any number of READ statements can occur in a program, in any place, and that in some programs involving loops it is necessary to use more than one READ statement to obtain the effect required (for instance, Example 1, page 40 of Book 3a). Obviously there must be enough data supplied to meet the requirements of the READ statements in the program.

2 Printing of numbers and text

In the sections on output we have shown how to print both numbers and words. The latter facility appeals to students and also helps in annotating output.

The commas in PRINT statements are extremely useful since they provide automatic tabulation across the page. With less able students it might be advisable to delay the introduction of the semi-colon as an alternative separator until a later stage.

Writing text should not cause any difficulty but notice that, if text and variables are mixed in the same PRINT statement, it is advisable that separators be placed between the various items since this is mandatory on many systems. For example,

```
10 PRINT "A =",A,"B =",B
```

The use of commas can also be very convenient when headings are required for tables. Statements such as

```
10 PRINT "HOURS","MINUTES"
        .  .  .  .  .  .  .  .  .  .  .  .  .  .
        .  .  .  .  .  .  .  .  .  .  .  .  .  .
        .  .  .  .  .  .  .  .  .  .  .  .  .  .
100 PRINT H,M
```

(where statement 100 is in a loop and produces a number of values of H and M) cause the values of H to lie in a column under HOURS and the values of M to lie in a column under MINUTES, because of the automatic tabulation.

3 Implementation of the READ statements

Suppose we have a program in which there are a number of READ statements and corresponding DATA statements. As the READ statements are executed, the numbers in the DATA statements are assigned in sequence to the variables occurring in the READ lists.

For example, with the program

```
10 READ A
20 READ B,C
    .  .  .  .  .  .
    .  .  .  .  .  .
50 READ E,F,G
    .  .  .  .  .  .
    .  .  .  .  .  .
100 READ H,K,L,M,N
    .  .  .  .  .  .
    .  .  .  .  .  .
    .  .  .  .  .  .
200 DATA 11,3,5,7,3,6,8
210 DATA 9,1,-1,0
      .  .  .  .  .  .  .  .
      .  .  .  .  .  .  .  .
```

A takes the value 11
B takes the value 3
C takes the value 5
E takes the value 7
F takes the value 3
. . . . .
M takes the value −1
N takes the value 0

We could regard the data as a list of numbers waiting to be read and could imagine an arrow pointing to the item in the list which is the next one to be read. At the start, the arrow points to the first item, 11. After the READ A statement this number has been read and the arrow moves to the number 3. After this number has been read into B, the arrow points to 5 and this goes into C, and so on.

The illustration below shows where the 'pointer' is at particular places in the program.

Pointer before any data are read	Pointer when number has been read into B but not yet into C	Pointer after 6 has been read into G but before 8 has been read into H	Pointer after all data have been read
→ 11	11	11	11
3	3	3	3
5	→ 5	5	5
7	7	7	7
3	3	3	3
6	6	6	6
8	8	→ 8	8
9	9	9	9
1	1	1	1
−1	−1	−1	−1
0	0	0	0
			→

It will be seen that the pointer moves down the list. If there are more data items than READ statements, the remaining numbers will be ignored. If there are too few data items, the computer detects the end of the list and reports an error.

4 Arithmetic expressions in PRINT statements

It is permissible to write arithmetic expressions in PRINT statements when this is convenient. This fact is mentioned in passing at a later stage of Book 3a but could be introduced whenever it is thought desirable.

The following example computes the sum and product of four numbers.

```
10 READ A,B,C,D
20 PRINT A+B+C+D,A*B*C*D
30 DATA 1,2,3,4
40 END
```

5 A particular use for the READ statement

In many programming problems there are numerical constants which need to be assigned to locations before the data which are being processed are read in. For example, a merchant may need to input the current price of his commodities before he can start processing his customers' orders. Separate READ and DATA statements to input these values at the start are very useful for this purpose.

Even if the prices were never changed, this form of input would obviate assignment statements of the type 10 LET A=14·65, 20 LET B=0·33, 30 LET C= 42·30, and so on. What is more probable is that the prices would change from time to time, in which case a new DATA card would provide the changes with no further alterations needed to the program.

The remainder of the program would contain further READ statements to handle customers' orders and would incorporate some means of repeating instructions in this part of the program without the need to re-read the initial data.

If the program were to be run interactively, the data on customer orders could be read in by using the INPUT statement. It is quite useful in this type of situation to be able to read the 'static' data by means of DATA statements and to use the INPUT statement for data which will be processed and then not required again.

6 Additional exercises

1. Write a program to read two numbers into A and B and to print column headings A, B, A+B, SQUARE OF A+B and the corresponding values beneath.
2. Write a program to read two numbers into A and B and to print out on separate lines:

    A=
    B=
    A+B=
    SQUARE OF A+B=

with the appropriate values given on the right-hand side of these expressions.
3. Write a program in which you read in as data your age (in years and months) and your date of birth (in the order day, month, year, e.g. 15 4 59), and print out the results in the following form:

    MY AGE IS ... YEARS ... MONTHS
    MY DATE OF BIRTH IS.../.../...

5 Loops

1 Introduction

We have chosen to introduce the subject of loops at an early stage of programming in order to demonstrate how easily the computer can repeatedly carry out a set of instructions and can continue to do so for as many times as required. In contrast to a human being it does not tire or start to make mistakes or even slow down just because it is doing the same thing many times.

2 The use of loops for repetitive operations

We would hope that the student would be impressed by the fact that in the following program (Book 3a, Chapter 5, page 37)

```
10 FOR I = 1 TO 75
20 READ L,W,H
30 LET V = L*W*H
40 PRINT V
50 NEXT I
60 DATA<STATEMENTS CONTAINING 3*75 NUMBERS>
70 END
```

he can calculate the volume of 75 boxes using a program of only half a dozen statements (plus his data) and, indeed, that by changing line 10 he can alter this number to any other he chooses within reason, i.e. within the largest number which can be held by the computer.

The teacher might like to point out that most big programs used commercially rely on loops. For instance, calculating the payroll for 1500 employees means repeating the same process 1500 times. The process is of course much more complex than the simple loops we use but the principle of repeated operations is the same.

3 The FOR statement and the counting variable

We use the FOR statement in its simplest form in this chapter and elaborate on it in

Chapter 8. It works in the following way: a count is set up in the location of the 'counting variable' (technically known as the *control variable*). Each time the NEXT statement is executed the count is increased by 1 and is then tested to see if it has yet exceeded the last value given in the FOR statement. If not, the statements sandwiched between the FOR and NEXT statements are repeated, the NEXT statement is again executed, 1 is added to the count and the test repeated. If the final value *has* been exceeded, the program continues to the statement that follows the NEXT statement. For example:

```
10 FOR I = 1 TO 5
20 . . . . . . . .
30 . . . . . . . .
40 . . . . . . . .
50 NEXT I
60 . . . . . . . .
```

No. of times round loop	Value of I after execution of line 50	Action after making the test I > 5
1	2	return to line 20
2	3	,, ,, ,, ,,
3	4	,, ,, ,, ,,
4	5	,, ,, ,, ,,
5	6	continue to line 60

The test for the end of the loop is also carried out when the loop is first entered, so that if we had the statement

```
10 FOR I = 1 TO 0
```

we should leave the loop immediately and go to line 60.

A simple analogy to counting in a loop is that of counting on your fingers, putting up one finger each time the 'statements' have been carried out and checking to see if the limit has been reached.

There is no particular magic about using the letter I for the counting variable. It is a normal location in the computer and any other valid name can be used instead. The letters I and J, however, are very frequently used for counting purposes.

4 Using a variable as a limit in the FOR statement

The major step forward in the chapter (section 4, page 39 of Book 3a) is the introduction of a variable as the upper limit to the count, i.e.

```
10 FOR I = 1 TO N
```

where N can be input as data. The advantage of being able to do this should be obvious. No longer is it necessary to change a program statement when a different-

31

sized loop is required: the same program will suffice. All that is needed is a statement such as

```
5 READ N
```

so that N has been given a value *before* the loop is set up.

Example

Write a program which calculates, for N sets of data, the number of minutes equivalent to a given number of hours and minutes and tabulates the results.

```
10 READ N
11 REM N IS THE NUMBER OF SETS
12 REM OF DATA TO BE READ
20 PRINT "HOURS","MINUTES","TOTAL MINUTES"
21 PRINT
30 FOR I = 1 TO N
40 READ H,M
50 LET T = H*60+M
60 PRINT H,M,T
70 NEXT I
80 DATA<VALUE OF N>
90 DATA<N SETS OF DATA>
100 END
```

5 Using the counting variable in the loop

Finally (section 5, page 41 of Book 3a), we have used the counting variable in the loop itself. There is no reason why this cannot be done, since it is a number stored in a normal location. It is obviously useful to be able to do this when the values we are calculating depend on the value of the counting variable, as in a tabulation.

A further important application occurs in Chapter 6 on lists, where we need the value of the counting variable to refer to particular items in the list.

We would also point out that it is in Chapter 5 (section 3, page 39 of Book 3a) that we have introduced the statement

```
40 LET S = S+A
```

where a running total is maintained in S, the value of S being increased by the quantity A each time the loop is executed.

6 Additional exercises

1. Twenty pupils sit an examination which has two sections A and B. Marks are awarded separately for each section. Write a program which reads these pairs of marks, first A and then B, for each pupil and calculates the average mark for sections A and B.

2. Fifteen motorists are used to test the petrol consumption of a new car. Each motorist calculates how many miles to the gallon he obtains when driving at 30 mi/h and how many he obtains when he drives at 50 mi/h. Write a program which takes

these two values for each motorist and calculates the average consumption obtained at both 30 mi/h and 50 mi/h.

3. Write a program capable of being used for both of the above problems.

4. (a) Write a program that calculates the sum

$$1+2+3+4+ \ldots +10$$

(b) Adapt the program so that it can calculate the sum

$$1+2+3+4+ \ldots +N$$

where N is given as data.

5. Write a similar program to that in question 4 to calculate

$$1^2+2^2+3^2+ \ldots +N^2$$

6. Write a program that will print the twelve-times table.

6 Lists

1 Introduction

Suppose we wish to compare the sales obtained by twenty salesmen during one week with those obtained during the previous week, and that the data available are two sets of twenty numbers each. We are then faced with the problem of storing forty numbers so that we can do the comparisons. Obviously, difficulties will arise over finding suitable names for the storage locations and in Book 3a we use this fact to introduce the need for lists—which will be easily understood.

The real purpose of using this (list) notation lies deeper, however, and one of its advantages is that we can use it to refer to all the elements of a list by means of a loop.

2 Elementary manipulation of list elements

In the early part of Chapter 6 we provide examples and exercises in manipulation of list elements. If the student has met subscripted variables in algebra, then an obvious analogy is available. (Some writers refer to list elements as 'subscripted variables'.) If not, it is sufficient to suggest that we are going to be working with a set of numbers all of the same kind (e.g. a number of items, ages, weights, and so on), and that it is convenient to give them an identifying name (letter) followed by an individual number. Naturally they will be numbered from 1 upwards.

3 Use of a variable as a subscript

We introduce the idea of using list elements in a loop by first showing that we can use a variable as a subscript. That is, we can write assignment statements containing expressions such as D(I), A(J), B(J+K). The values of I, J and K at the time when the statements are executed determine which element of the appropriate list is used. It follows that by writing

```
50 FOR I = 1 TO 10
60 PRINT A(I)
70 NEXT I
```

the elements A(1), A(2), A(3), . . ., A(10) of the list A would be printed out in turn.

4 Loops and lists

Lists are frequently used in association with loops. In most cases the elements of a list are also elements of a set and very often we want to examine all the elements of the set to find some particular property. For example,

Which salesman sold the largest number of items?
How many people travelled more than a given distance?
Is there any one in the set under 21 years of age?
What is the average weight of the members of the set?

We anticipate later chapters by posing these questions here, since we have not yet shown how decisions are taken. However, simpler examples based on the salesmen problem (mentioned earlier) can easily illustrate the point.

If we have sales figures from twenty salesmen for the past week and the corresponding figures for the present week, the following piece of program reads the first set of figures into a list P and the second into a list W. The dimension statement at the beginning of the program makes available another list R in which we might want to put results.

```
10 DIM P(20),W(20),R(20)
20 FOR I = 1 TO 20
30 READ P(I)
40 NEXT I
50 FOR I = 1 TO 20
60 READ W(I)
70 NEXT I
80 . . .
```

We can add up the sales for a fortnight for each salesman with the loop

```
80 FOR I = 1 TO 20
90 LET R(I) = P(I)+W(I)
100 NEXT I
```

or we can find which salesmen have improved their sales in the second week by doing a subtraction:

```
80 FOR I = 1 TO 20
90 LET R(I) = W(I)-P(I)
100 NEXT I
```

On printing the values of R(I), positive values indicate increased sales.

It is only by using a loop and a variable subscript that we are able to modify the location we are examining and thus easily repeat the operation on all elements of the list.

Notice that in this example and in some examples in Book 3a we have used more than one loop in the program. The loops are quite separate, however, and do not lie inside each other. (We deal with this more complicated problem at the end of Chapter 8.) Once a loop has been completed we have finished counting and the same control variable can be legitimately used in a second loop later in the program.

5 Subscript checking

We do not mention in Book 3a what happens if the subscript in the list element exceeds the value given in the DIM statement, that is if we have

```
10 DIM A(20)
20 LET I = 21
30 LET A(I) = 0
```

The computer accepts the above statements as valid **BASIC** but when the program is run a check is made on subscript values and an error message is printed to say that a subscript has been used which is 'out of bounds'. The program is then abandoned. Negative subscripts are not allowed and would also be trapped during a run of the program with an 'out of bounds' message.

We have implied that DIM A(20) makes available to the user the list elements A(1), A(2), ..., A(20). In fact, the element A(0) is also available in some systems but, since counting usually starts at 1, we have omitted this information from Book 3a.

We have also omitted to mention that for lists with ten or less elements it is not essential to provide a DIM statement. We do not like this facility for a number of reasons:

1. The facility is not available in other languages.
2. Lists with ten or less elements are treated differently from larger ones.
3. Without a DIM statement the computer assumes a list of ten elements, thus wasting space when the list used is not large.
4. Any subscript up to ten is taken as valid, even when the list is shorter.

6 Additional exercises

1. Eight judges are judging an ice-skating contest and they award marks for technical ability and artistic interpretation. Write a program which reads the first set of marks into a list T, the second set into a list A, and then calculates the two average marks.
2. A motor salesman sells two versions of the same car, the deluxe model and the super deluxe. Each week he records the number of each type of car he has sold. At the end of a year he puts into the computer the pairs of numbers he has obtained. Write a program which will read in these pairs of numbers and will calculate:
   (i) the total number of cars of each type sold
   (ii) the average number of cars of each type sold per week
   (iii) the total number of cars sold each week
   (iv) the grand total of all cars sold during the year.
3. A manufacturer makes a particular shirt in six sizes, 1–6, and the price is slightly different for each size. He stores in the computer in a list P the price of each shirt, so that P(1) contains the price of the size 1 shirt, P(2) contains the price of the size 2 shirt, and so on. He then processes each customer's order by putting in as data the number of shirts of each size which the customer requires. For example, 3, 4, 2, 1, 0, 0 would indicate that the customer wanted 3 shirts of size 1, 4 shirts of size 2, 2 shirts of size 3, 1 shirt of size 4 and no shirts of size 5 or 6. Write a program which will read in these six numbers, multiply them by the appropriate price and calculate the total cost of the order.

7 Jumps

1 Introduction

When we write loops we jump back in the program to allow certain statements to be executed again. In this chapter we show how we can make jumps to other parts of a program. Our programs may now contain *branch points* at which different courses of action can be taken.

Logically the techniques of jumps should be introduced before loops, since we can construct our own loops from jump instructions but not vice versa. We introduced loops first because they are an easier concept and demonstrate effectively the power of the computer.

2 The computer's power to discriminate

The computer gained its early reputation for being an 'electronic brain' because of its ability to discriminate between values. The decision-making process consists basically of the computer being able to compare two numbers. In a language such as BASIC this facility has been incorporated into *conditional statements* of the form

```
10 IF A>B THEN 120
```

where two arithmetic expressions are compared. If the relationship is true then a jump to the statement number following the THEN is made, otherwise the next statement following the conditional statement is executed.

In this chapter we introduce the decision box into flow charts and from now on more extensive use is made of flow charts. Programs are no longer necessarily executed sequentially and it is helpful to the student to draw flow charts to see the action of the program. Besides the conditional statement we also introduce the *unconditional* jump which is of the form

```
10 GOTO 150
```

where a jump to the appropriate statement is *always* made.

We have limited our examples in this chapter to those using only one conditional statement so that an understanding of the statement is obtained before it is used in more complex situations where analysis of the problem becomes the more important factor.

3 Flow charts involving decisions

The basic flow charts associated with the conditional statement are:

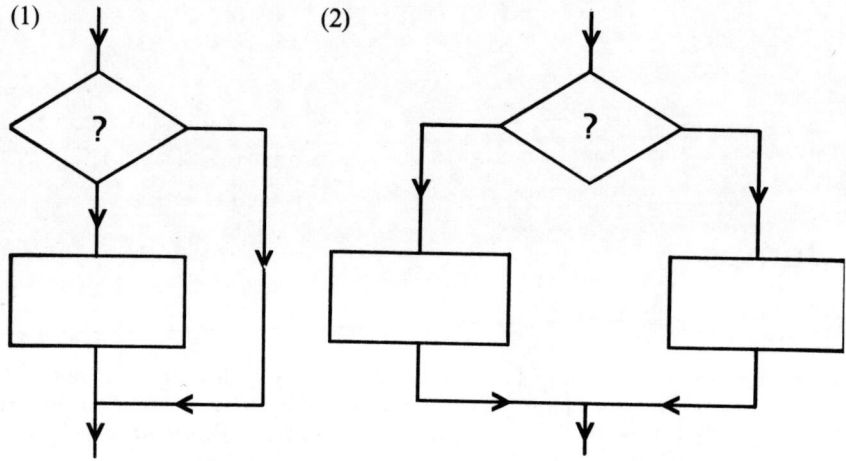

In (1), the program is rejoined after the omission of a few statements. In (2), each branch contains one or more statements. The two branches may join up again or may contain completely different material, only joining up at the END statement.

Jumps may be made in either a forward or backward direction. To keep matters simple there is no illustration of the latter in Book 3a but an example of its use occurs in the following program:

```
10 LET S = 0
20 LET N = 0
30 IF N=20 THEN 80
40 READ A
50 LET S = S+A
60 LET N = N+1
70 GOTO 30
80 PRINT S
90 DATA<20 NUMBERS>
100 END
```

with the corresponding flow chart:

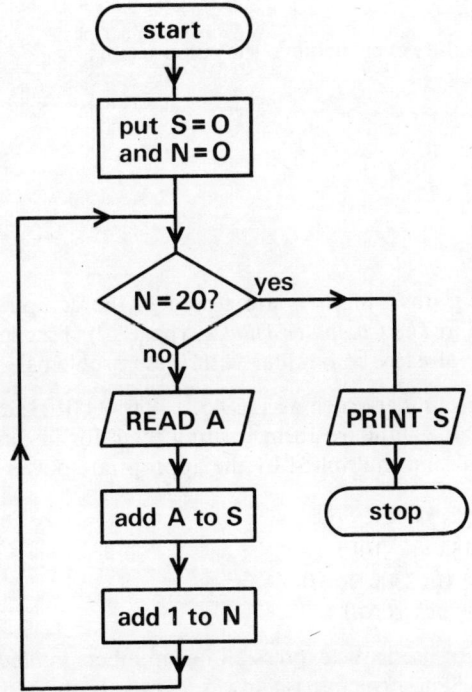

The reader will observe that the program goes round a loop (lines 30 to 70). A count is maintained in N and 1 is added to this (line 60) each time round. The test in line 30 is true after twenty cycles of the loop have been completed. The program then jumps to line 80 and finishes.

This example shows how we can construct our own loops without needing to utilise the FOR statement.

4 Notation for comparison symbols

We have used the standard notations for the symbols used in comparisons. Some systems use alternative notations for the symbols $<=$, $>=$, $<>$, such as LE, GE, NE.

5 More general relations

The items on each side of the comparison symbols can be arithmetic expressions of the form discussed in Chapter 3. We could, for instance, write

```
10 IF B*B>4*A*C THEN 100
```

or

```
20 IF ABS(A-B)<0.005 THEN 110
```

but in practice simple variables are most frequently used.

39

It is not permissible to write conditions involving more than one comparison. That is,

```
10  IF  A<B<C  THEN  120
```

is not allowed. The following two tests, however, achieve the same result:

```
10  IF  A<B  THEN  50
 o   o   o   •   o   •   •   •
 •   o   o   •   •   •   o   o
50  IF  B<C  THEN  120
```

6 Floating point arithmetic

In Book 3a we have avoided describing how numbers are stored in the computer. Information on this subject is contained in *The Computer Thinks?* (page 29), Teachers' Book 1b of this series, so that you may already be familiar with these problems.

Briefly, we have the problem of storing numbers such as 123·45, 1·456, 0·00123, and so on. We can reduce them all to the same standard form, writing them for instance as a number following the decimal point and multiplied by the appropriate power of 10, so that we get:

$$123·45 = 0·12345 \times 1000 = 0·12345 \times 10^3$$
$$1·456 = 0·14560 \times 10 = 0·14560 \times 10^1$$
$$0·00123 = 0·12300 \times 1/100 = 0·12300 \times 10^{-2}$$

(The digit following the decimal point is not zero.)

In the computer, decimal numbers are not used. We express all our numbers in *binary* form, i.e. using only the digits 0 and 1. The principle is, however, exactly the same. All numbers can be reduced to a standard form in which a numeric value is multiplied by the appropriate power of 2. When numbers are in this form it is much easier for the computer to do arithmetic with them. Such arithmetic is known as *floating point arithmetic* and the number itself as a *floating point number*.

The user needs to know little about the mechanism involved in doing this arithmetic. He puts his numbers into the computer in decimal form, the conversions are done automatically for him and after the computation is completed his results are converted back to decimal before being printed.

One slight difficulty might arise, which we also encounter in ordinary decimal arithmetic. We write $\frac{2}{3}$ in decimal as 0·666667. This is a continuing decimal and we have to cut it short at some point and approximate to the result. We do this by rounding up the last digit to 7. Similarly, we write $\frac{1}{3}$ in decimal as 0·333333, which is also an approximation since this decimal continues for ever. If we now multiply $\frac{1}{3}$ by 2 we get 0·666666. Thus, we have shown that $2 \times \frac{1}{3}$ is not equal to $\frac{2}{3}$, there being a difference of 1 in the sixth decimal place. The reason for this, of course, is the approximations which we had to make because we used only a finite number (6) of decimal places.

Exactly the same problem may occur in the computer. The accuracy of a number will be limited by the length of the word in the computer store and slight rounding errors may occur. This means that if we have numbers in two locations A and B which we think are the same, they may differ slightly because of some calculation that has been done.

In the IF statement

```
10 IF A=B THEN 100
```

the computer will test A and B to see if they are *exactly* the same (i.e. if they each have the same binary pattern). If not, then the test will not succeed. We may indeed find the test failing when we expect it to succeed. It is therefore unwise to test for the equality of two floating point numbers.

This situation does not arise when integers are being compared, since these can be represented accurately and do not need to be turned into floating point form. (Some implementations of BASIC, however, turn all numbers, including integers, into floating point numbers but even here problems seldom arise with integers, since they are usually sufficiently small to be represented accurately.)

To deal with the problem of comparing two floating point numbers we have to be more definite about what we mean by 'equal' in any particular situation. For instance, we may be satisfied that A and B are equal if they differ by less than 0·0001. In this case what we are saying is that A—B must lie between —0·0001 and +0·0001. Another way to put this is ABS (A—B) < 0·0001 and the 'equality' statement can be rewritten as

```
10 IF ABS(A-B)<0.0001 THEN 100
```

We would suggest that most students will not encounter this difficulty, since their problems are usually of an integer nature. The more adventurous student may meet it, however, and the above explanation and technique will be of value.

7 Additional exercises

1. An Electricity Board charges 6p per unit for the first 200 units used in a three monthly period and 1·3p per unit thereafter. Write a program that reads as data the meter readings at the beginning and end of the period and calculates the cost of the electricity.
2. Write a program to read three numbers A, B and C and to calculate and print $\sqrt{(B^2-4AC)}$. Before the square root is taken, write a test to see if B^2-4AC is negative. If it is, do not calculate the square root, but print instead NEGATIVE VALUE.
3. A company makes equipment used by business firms for copying documents. The company provides a firm with a machine and charges it 2·5p for each copy made. At the end of each month, a meter shows how many copies have been made. Write a program which calculates what the monthly charge should be. There is a minimum charge of £20 per month. Write the program so that it prints the total number of copies made and the charge which the company makes.
4. A company allows expenses for running a car at the rate of 4p per kilometre for cars under 1300 cm³ and 4·5p per kilometre for cars of greater cubic capacity. Write a program which reads as data the cubic capacity of the car, followed by the distance travelled on a journey, and gives as the result the expenses which can be claimed for the journey.

8 More jumps and loops

1 Introduction

In this chapter we increase the complexity of the logic behind the programs and end by combining both jumps and loops.

2 Exit from a loop

Initially we show how an exit can be made from a continuous cycle of instructions by means of a conditional statement. The example used is one which occurs frequently in practice. In many instances when data have to be input to a program, it is not known beforehand how much information is available. In these circumstances it is not possible to set up a loop using a FOR statement. Instead, the data have to be read in item by item using a GOTO statement to return to the READ statement so that the next item is read.

```
10 READ A
   .  .  .  .
   .  .  .  .
   .  .  .  .
50 GOTO 10
```

Eventually the execution of the READ statement will fail because there are no more data.

To overcome this difficulty we do two things. First, we include an extra item at the end of the data which is obviously different from the actual data being processed. Secondly, we introduce a test immediately after the READ statement so that this extra item, which identifies the end of the data, can be found and a jump made to another part of the program.

Example

In the following program a set of positive numbers is read and their mean is calculated.

The set is terminated by a negative number and this causes a jump from the loop. The running total is calculated in S and the number of numbers read is counted in N.

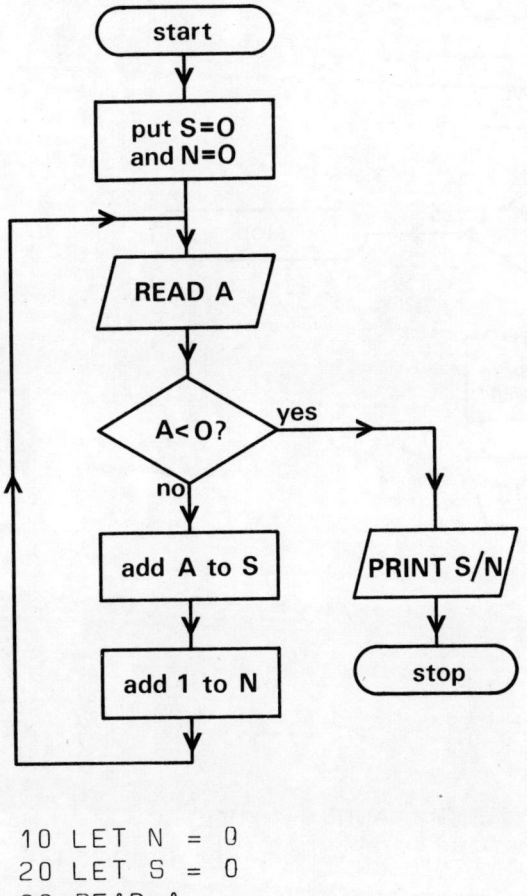

```
10 LET N = 0
20 LET S = 0
30 READ A
40 IF A<0 THEN 80
50 LET S = S+A
60 LET N = N+1
70 GOTO 30
80 PRINT S/N
90 DATA<SET OF POSITIVE NUMBERS
           ENDING WITH A NEGATIVE>
100 END
```

Note that if both positive and negative numbers occur as data, then it is usually possible to find some numbers out of range which can be used as a terminator to the data, e.g. 999999 or some such large number.

In the flow chart and program occurring on page 59 of Book 3a, viz.

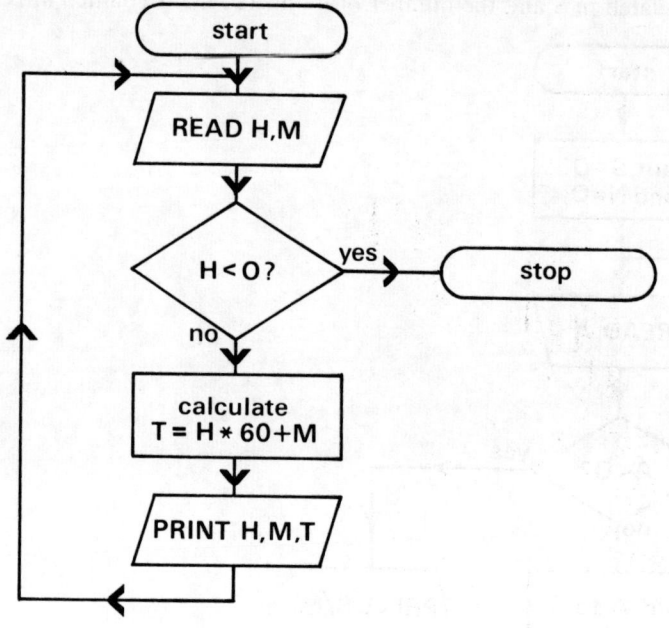

```
10 READ H,M
20 IF H<0 THEN 70
30 LET T = H*60+M
40 PRINT H,M,T
50 GOTO 10
60 DATA<SETS OF HOURS AND MINUTES
        ENDING WITH TWO NEGATIVE NUMBERS>
70 END
```

we remark that the true data must be terminated by two negative numbers. These two numbers go into H and M, and whilst it is not essential that M should be negative (since it is not examined) it is necessary for two numbers to be provided in order to complete the READ statement.

An alternative way of drawing the flow chart and of writing the program so that only one item is needed to terminate the data is:

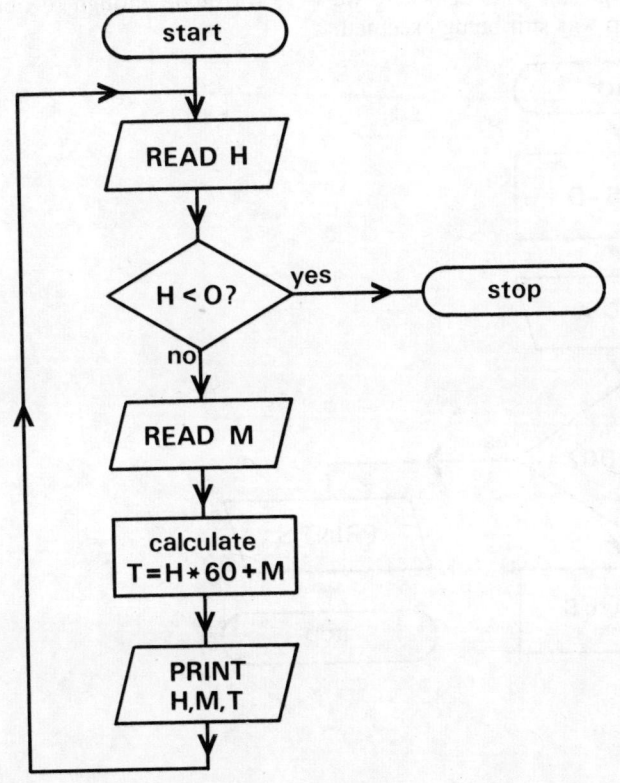

```
10 READ H
20 IF H<0 THEN 70
25 READ M
30 LET T = H*60+M
40 PRINT H,M,T
50 GOTO 10
60 DATA<SET OF HOURS AND MINUTES
        ENDING WITH ONE NEGATIVE>
70 END
```

This version has little else to commend it since it doubles the number of times that the READ statement has to be used.

We should also point out that it is implicit in the program that the sets of numbers to be converted occur in pairs. If an exact number of hours (say 6) were to be converted, this would need to be written as the pair 6,0 and if a value of, say, 45 minutes were to be converted, this would be written as 0,45.

The following example from section 4, page 60 of Book 3a, finds the sum of a given set of numbers. A result is not obtained until an exit has been made from the loop, in contrast to the first example on page 58 where we were fortunate enough to obtain our results whilst the loop was still being executed.

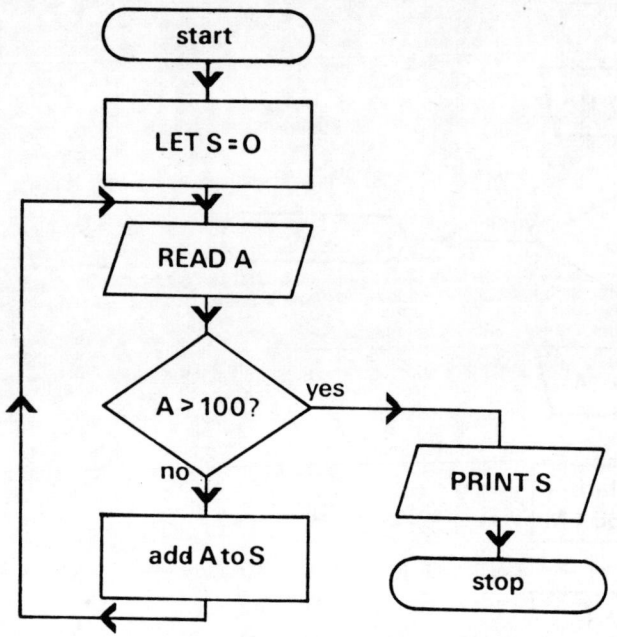

```
10 LET S = 0
20 READ A
30 IF A>100 THEN 60
40 LET S = S+A
50 GOTO 20
60 PRINT S
70 DATA<SET OF NUMBERS ENDING WITH
        A NUMBER BIGGER THAN 100>
80 END
```

3 More than one decision box

On page 61 of Book 3a we introduce the idea that we can make more than one decision during a program. Example 1 is a program to print out the values of numbers of a set which are greater than or equal to 10. The set of numbers is terminated by the number −999.

The flow diagram associated with the program is:

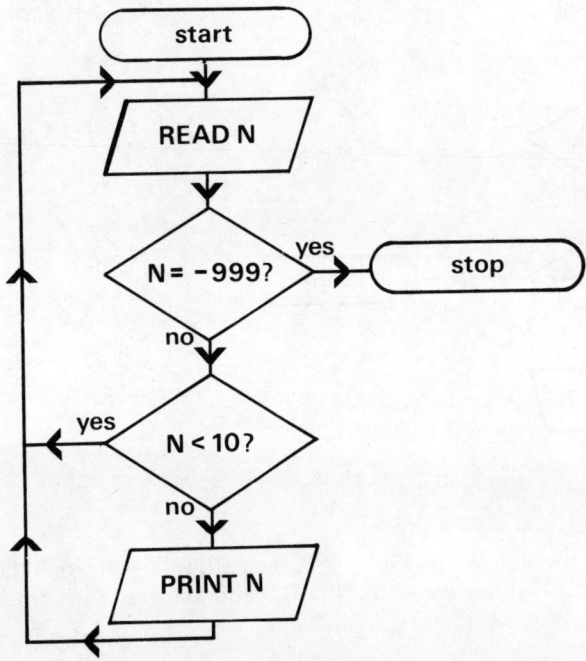

This kind of situation, where we want to carry out some test on valid data and use another test to find the end of data, occurs very frequently.

We comment in Book 3a that each item read is tested to see if it is the end of data. It may appear stupid to have to test for the end of data on the first item read, since we would not expect it to be the terminator, but it is easier to do this than to write a special piece of program to deal separately with the first item. In any case, the program should in fact be able to handle this peculiar situation if it were to arise. One such situation might be as follows. In a bank, the total in each customer's account is calculated after each deposit or withdrawal. If the account is liable to become overdrawn a message must be printed to this effect before the withdrawal causing the overdraft is computed. That is, if the amount to be withdrawn is more than the present balance, a message must be printed. In this situation we must trap the customer who makes a withdrawal before any deposits, i.e. when the first data item causes the message to be printed.

Referring to the flow diagram for the original problem, we see that the test for 'end of data' occurs as soon as the data item has been read. This is to ensure that such a number is not processed. If instead we had used the diagram

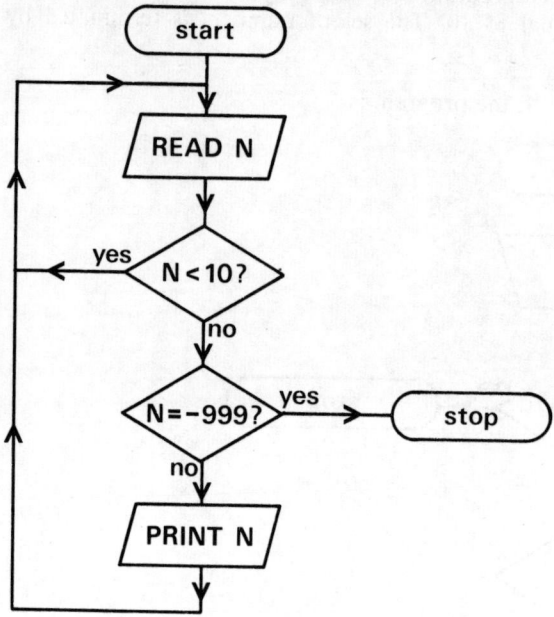

we would never have reached the end. With N = −999, the path followed would have gone along the 'yes' branch of the first decision (N < 10?) and the test to jump out of the loop would never have been satisfied.

This is an example of an incorrectly designed solution to the problem. Even if correct BASIC statements corresponding to this last flow diagram were written, there would be no hope of obtaining correct answers from it.

One final criticism we might make of the original flow diagram is that, if by chance all the numbers we were testing were less than 10, we would have no print-out and we might then have some doubts as to whether or not the program was working satisfactorily and had come to its proper end. To get round this difficulty it is advisable to ask for some sort of print-out from each branch of the program. In this case the addition of a PRINT statement (as shown opposite) would be advantageous.

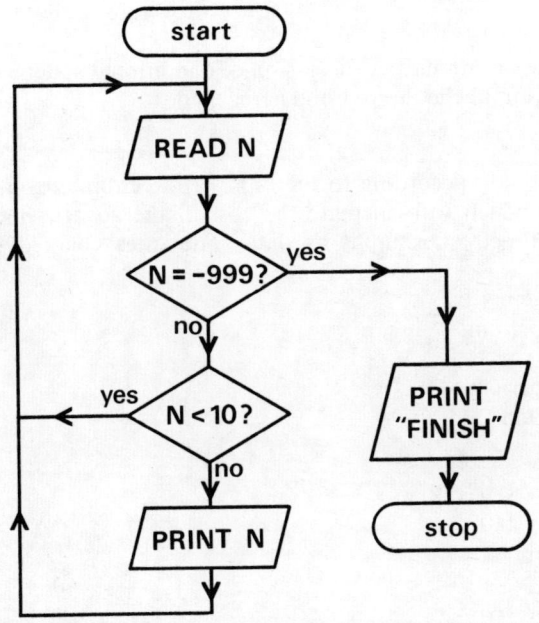

Example 2, on page 62 of Book 3a, whose program is

```
10 READ Y,M
20 LET A = Y*12+M
30 IF A<72 THEN 100
40 IF A>144 THEN 100
50 PRINT A
60 GOTO 120
100 PRINT "OUT OF RANGE"
110 DATA<AGE IN YEARS & MONTHS>
120 END
```

is included to show that we can jump to the same statement from different parts of the program. That is, we may jump to line 100 either from line 30 or from line 40. Example 3 (page 64 of Book 3a) shows how to keep a count by using the statement

```
50 LET N = N+1
```

and Example 4 (page 65) reiterates the technique for keeping a running total.

4 Multiple decisions

The following example shows how we can have a succession of conditional statements gradually filtering out possibilities until the desired one is reached.

Example

The advertising rates in a journal vary according to the number of centimetres used in the column. Write a program which will calculate the cost of the advertisement when its length (in column centimetres) is input as data. The rates charged for advertisements are:

1 to 15 cm	£7 per cm
16 to 35 cm	£6·50 per cm
36 to 65 cm	£6 per cm
66 to 105 cm	£5·50 per cm
106 cm or more	£5 per cm

```
10 READ L
15 IF L<0 THEN 160
20 IF L>15 THEN 50
30 PRINT "£";7*L
40 GOTO 10
50 IF L>35 THEN 80
60 PRINT "£";6.50*L
70 GOTO 10
80 IF L>65 THEN 110
90 PRINT "£";6*L
100 GOTO 10
110 IF L>105 THEN 140
120 PRINT "£";5.50*L
130 GOTO 10
140 PRINT "£";5*L
150 GOTO 10
160 PRINT "FINISHED"
170 DATA 4,17,37,67,123,15,35,65
180 DATA 105,3,16,36,66,106,-1
190 END
```

5 Using jumps in FOR statements

Sections 7 and 8 (pages 66-70 of Book 3a) show how jumps and loops can be incorporated within loops generated by FOR statements. In Example 5 (page 66) we read N numbers in a loop. Within each cycle of the loop we test to see if the number is negative or non-negative and keep a count in either case. Having done this we need to go round the loop again. The way to do this is to go to the NEXT I statement since this provides an automatic return to the beginning of the loop, updating the count as it does so.

The relevant program statements in Example 5 are:

```
40 FOR I = 1 TO N
50 READ A
60 IF A<0 THEN 90
70 LET P = P+1
80 GOTO 100
90 LET Q = Q+1
100 NEXT I
```

If $A<0$, statements 90 and 100 are obeyed; if $A>=0$, statements 70, 80 and 100 are obeyed.

Notice that if we try to go back to the beginning of the loop by writing GOTO 50, I will not be incremented and the count will be wrong. We commit an even graver error if we write GOTO 40, since this would set up the loop from the beginning again.

In the example just quoted the GOTO statement led to another statement contained *in* the loop (i.e. lying between lines 50 and 100 inclusive) but Example 6 (page 69 of Book 3a) shows how a jump can be made *from* a loop. When a jump is made out of a loop, the value of the counting variable is available to the programmer. It is in fact the current value of I (or whatever variable name was used for the loop). It is often convenient to use the value of the count in conjunction with the jump out of a loop, as is suggested in Exercise 6, question 1 on page 70 of Book 3a.

6 A further example

The following mathematical example uses the same principle.

Find how many terms of the series
$$1 + \tfrac{1}{2} + \tfrac{1}{3} + \tfrac{1}{4} + \tfrac{1}{5} + \tfrac{1}{6} + \cdots$$
have to be added together before the sum exceeds the value 5.

The program is:

```
10 LET S = 0
20 FOR I = 1 TO 500
30 LET S = S+1/I
40 IF S>5 THEN 70
50 NEXT I
60 PRINT "EXIT FROM LOOP"
70 PRINT "SUM =";S,"NO OF TERMS =";I
80 END
```

It has several interesting points. The counting variable is used inside the loop to generate the necessary terms. If the condition in line 40 is satisfied a jump is made to line 70 where the number of terms (equal to I) is printed.

We try to choose an upper value of I that is sufficiently high so that line 40 will be satisfied before all the cycles in the loop have been made. We may however make a poor guess and to protect ourselves we have inserted a warning message in line 60 to report that we have completed the loop and have 'come out at the bottom' instead of by the conditional statement. Whilst in our particular example the value of S would show that we had not completed our task, in many more complex problems we might continue in ignorance of the mistakes we were perpetrating if we had no such warning. However, we would advise against setting the upper value of the count as high as possible, since this could waste a great deal of computer time if for some reason the program or logic were wrong.

It can be shown that the sum

$$1 + \tfrac{1}{2} + \tfrac{1}{3} + \tfrac{1}{4} + \tfrac{1}{5} + \tfrac{1}{6} + \ldots$$

can be made as large as we like provided that we add on a sufficient number of terms. It takes nearly two million terms to reach the value 15, so the question of how many terms are required to reach, say, 100 leads to such astronomical figures that the computer could not handle these without special programming.

This example suggests that we might even use the loop as a means of control so that, if something does go wrong with our calculations, we will be able to come to a stop after a given number of cycles.

We would also point out that, whilst we suggested using jumps inside loops and jumps from loops, we have nowhere indicated that jumps can be made *into* loops from outside. Entry into loops must be through the FOR statement.

7 Change of step length

In all the examples quoted up to this point we have used loops in which increments are made in steps of 1. We can, however, change this incremental step by adding to the FOR statement the step length we desire.

The statement

```
10 FOR I = 1 TO 19 STEP 2
```

will increase I in steps of 2. That is, it gives I successively the values 1, 3, 5, . . ., 17, 19.

In the statement

```
10 FOR I = 1 TO 20 STEP 2
```

I takes the same values and the loop is terminated when I has reached 19. The fact that in the statement I ranges from 1 to 20 does not affect the issue since the next value I could take would be 21. Since this is greater than 20 the loop is terminated.

It is not necessary for the step length to be an integer, as shown in the statement (in Example 7, page 73 of Book 3a):

```
30 FOR L = 0.1 TO 10 STEP 0.1
```

In fact, the three values in the FOR statement may be variables or even arithmetic expressions.

```
10 FOR X = A TO B STEP C
```

and

```
20 FOR P = X*X TO Y*Y
```

are permitted.

The step length may be negative. We can write, for example:

```
10 FOR Z = 5 TO 3 STEP -0.2
```

8 Counting in non-integer steps

We went to some lengths at the end of Chapter 7 to show how comparison of equalities between floating point numbers could lead to difficulties because of rounding errors. The same situation may arise in FOR statements, particularly when non-integer steps are taken. For example, in the loop

```
10 FOR X = 1 TO 50 STEP 0.1
```

X is being incremented by 0·1 five hundred times. It is quite possible that rounding errors will build up so that in the last cycle the value of X may be, say, 49·99999 or 50·00001. The difference will be very slight and for most computational purposes the value of 49·99999 is near enough to 50 to make no significant difference to the result —if it does, the user should be learning something about approximation theory!

If the value of X has risen to 50·00001 a different situation arises. This value is greater than 50, so the loop will not be executed on the last occasion. It might happen then, for instance, that the last item in a table is not calculated. We can prevent this from happening by altering the FOR statement slightly. Instead of giving the upper limit exactly, we put in a value slightly above this. If we add *half* of the step length to the final value, this will ensure that the final cycle is executed but not an additional one.

The FOR statement in our example would become

```
10 FOR X = 1 TO 50.05 STEP 0.1
```

Once again, we would suggest that this particular problem is not brought to the attention of students unless it arises in practice.

9 Loops inside loops

We finish Chapter 8 in Book 3a by showing how one loop can be 'nested' inside another. We first write a program containing a loop and then enclose these program statements in another loop so that the inner program is repeated five times as shown below.

```
10 FOR B = 1 TO 5
20 LET T = 0
30 FOR I = 1 TO 4
40 READ D
50 LET T = T+D
60 NEXT I
70 PRINT T
80 NEXT B
90 DATA<4 DISTANCES FOR EACH OF 5 BOYS>
100 END
```

This is a very simple example of using one loop inside another since the counting variables are not used in the computations. An important application for using nested loops occurs in Chapter 9 when we want to refer to items in a table (i.e. a list with two subscripts). In referring to tables we use the values of the counting variables to identify the particular element of the table required.

It should be noted that when using nested loops one loop lies completely within the other. It is correct to write

```
50 FOR I = 1 TO M
  . . . . . . . .
  . . . . . . . .
100 FOR J = 1 TO N
  . . . . . . . .
  . . . . . . . .
150 NEXT J
  . . . . . .
  . . . . . .
170 NEXT I
```

and to nest loops three deep (or even more), e.g.

```
20 FOR I = 1 TO M
30 FOR J = 1 TO N
40 FOR K = 1 TO P
  . . . . . . . .
  . . . . . . . .
120 NEXT K
130 NEXT J
140 NEXT I
```

but we are not allowed to write

```
20 FOR I = 1 TO N
  . . . . . . . . .
40 FOR J = 1 TO M
  . . . . . . . . .
60 NEXT I
  . . . . . .
80 NEXT J
```

since this interlinks the 'I' and 'J' loops.

We conclude by writing a program in which we make use of the value of the counting variables in the loops. The following program prints in adjacent columns the one-, two-, three- and four-times tables.

```
10 FOR I = 1 TO 10
20 PRINT
30 FOR J = 1 TO 4
40 PRINT I*J,
50 NEXT J
60 NEXT I
70 END
```

On entry to the program, I is set to 1 and a new line is printed by line 20. At line 30 J is initially set to 1. Line 40 prints the product I*J=1. The statement NEXT J causes a return in the inner loop, J is set to 2 and the product I*J=2 is now printed. This continues up to the value J=4. Since there is a comma at the end of line 40 the four values 1, 2, 3, 4 are all printed on the same line.

At the end of the inner loop we go to line 60, thus causing a return in the outer loop. This increases the value of I to 2, the PRINT statement in line 20 provides a new line, and on entering the inner loop again the product now gives in turn the values 2, 4, 6, 8, since I has the value 2 and J runs through the values 1, 2, 3 and 4. The remainder of the table is output as I takes successively the values 3, 4, . . ., 9, 10.

We have included in Book 3a a similar explanation of output when we show how to print out the contents of a table.

10 Additional exercises

1. Goods in a warehouse are marked with a code number and a price. If the code number is 200 or less then VAT is not charged on the article: otherwise a charge of 10% is added. Write a program to print out the total cost of a number of goods purchased and the VAT charged. The data to be read consist of pairs of numbers, the first representing the code number of the article and the second its cost. The data are terminated by two negative numbers.

2. Write a program which will read the time in hours and minutes from a 24-hour clock and will print the time in 12-hour form adding A.M. or P.M. to the output as necessary.

3. An Electricity Board charges the following rates to domestic users:

     for the first 100 units used — 3·3p per unit
     for the next 300 units used — 1·5p per unit
     for further units used   — 0·9p per unit

Write a program which reads as data the number of units a user has consumed and calculates the cost of the electricity.

4. An apparatus measures the concentration of a certain biochemical substance in the blood and gives as a result a numerical value between 1 and 40. Write a program which reads a set of these numbers (terminated by a negative number), counts the number of numbers in each of the categories 1–10, 11–20, 21–30, 31–40, and finally prints these totals with appropriate text.

5. A football manager, analysing his team's performance after playing thirty matches, wishes to know the total number of goals scored and the goal average at the end of each successive match. Write a program which reads as data the number of goals scored in each match (in order of playing) and prints out a table giving on each line the number of matches played, the total goals scored and the goal average.

6. There are twenty-eight contestants in a competition and each is given a number. The mark which they obtain in the competition is written against this number. Write a program which will read these pairs of numbers (contestant number first, followed by the mark) and will

     (i) print out the number and mark of any contestant who scores 80 or more
     (ii) calculate and print the average mark
     (iii) print out the number of the contestant who has scored the highest mark, and his mark. (You may assume that not more than one competitor will come out top.)

7. Write a program to discover how many terms of the series
$$1+4+9+16+25+36+ \ldots$$
have to be added together for the sum to exceed a total of 1000.

8. The stopping distance (in metres) of a car on dry roads is calculated from the formula:
$$\text{stopping distance} = 0 \cdot 2V + 0 \cdot 006V^2$$
where V is the speed of the car in kilometres per hour. Write a program to produce a table of stopping distances for speeds ranging from 10 to 150 kilometres per hour in steps of 10 kilometres per hour.

9. Write a program to print a table of the squares and cubes of the numbers 1·0, 1·1, 1·2, . . ., 3·9, 4·0, putting appropriate headings at the top of the columns.

10. Generalise the above program to allow a table of squares and cubes to be printed starting with a value A and ending with a value B, the incremental step having a value H where A, B and H are read into the program as data.

9 Problem solving using lists and tables

1 Retaining information in lists

The first problem is that of reading a list of data items (sales of records) to find the average and then examining the deviations from the average value. The important point to notice is that we *must* retain all our data since, having calculated the average, we refer back to each item in turn. In fact, whenever data have to be rescanned, all the data must be kept available and the list is the usual way to do this.

2 Lists of varying lengths

In the second problem (page 77 of Book 3a), we deal with lists containing variable numbers of items, viz. the number of pupils in a class. We use a list large enough to accommodate the longest lists we are likely to encounter and then use only the first N of these elements. This is clearly acceptable since the loop FOR I=1 TO N will access only the first N elements of the list and we are not interested in what lies in the elements with subscripts N+1, and so on.

There may be a temptation to try to define the dimension of a list by DIM(N) where N is a value input to the program. This unfortunately is not permissible. Only integers are allowed in dimension statements. We must therefore settle on an appropriate maximum size for the list before starting to use it.

In the same example we show an arithmetic expression being used in a PRINT statement. The expression is evaluated in the usual way and then the final value is printed. There is no reason why this idea should not be introduced at an earlier stage of teaching if it is thought desirable.

When the computer accesses an element in a list, it first has to be told which list it has to access and then which element it has to find. These two steps take more time than that required to access an ordinary simple variable. The pedant might thus object to the two statements

```
50 READ P(I)
60 LET S = S+P(I)
```

and prefer to replace them with

```
50 READ W
60 LET S = S+W
65 LET P(I) = W
```

Here, by storing our value temporarily in W, we can save one reference to the list. Obviously, the time saved is negligible in the type of programs we shall be writing but in programs where many thousands or even millions of accesses to lists and tables are made, the savings can be considerable.

These comments show how good technique can improve the efficient running of programs. It is not, however, a point we would labour with the students.

3 The problem of finding the largest number in a list

We explain in more detail in section 3 (page 78 of Book 3a) how a list can be scanned for the largest element in the list. The technique is to scan the list and store in a location M the largest value yet encountered. If in the search a bigger value is found than that already in M, then this new value is put into M, replacing the old one. Since the whole list is scanned systematically we end up with the largest element of the list in M. Notice that we have to give M an initial value to start with, otherwise an error will occur if M is never replaced.

In the exercise which follows (Exercise 1, question 2, page 80 of Book 3a), we suggest that the position of the smallest element of the list can be found by putting into a location P the corresponding value of I whenever a new 'smallest' value goes into M.

This technique for scanning a list is frequently used. In combination with keeping a count, for instance, it can be used to find the number of elements of a list which possess a given property (e.g. how many elements of a list are zero).

4 The problem of comparing lists

The examples in section 4 (page 81 of Book 3a) emphasise that more than one list may be used in a program and that the order in which data are input is dependent on how the program is written. For example,

```
20 FOR I = 1 TO 12
30 READ A(I)
40 NEXT I
50 FOR I = 1 TO 12
60 READ B(I)
70 NEXT I
```

implies that the first twelve data items go into list A and the next twelve into list B.

The program segment

```
20 FOR I = 1 TO 12
30 READ A(I),B(I)
40 NEXT I
```

implies that data are input in pairs so that the first item goes to A(1), the second to B(1), the third to A(2), the fourth to B(2), and so on.

5 Tables

Sections 5 and 6 (pages 82–84 of Book 3a) introduce the concept of a table, which is a two-dimension list. That is, we are dealing with a variable which has two subscripts. If we imagine a tabular lay-out as indicated below

1,1	1,2	1,3	1,4	1,5
2,1	2,2	2,3	2,4	2,5
3,1	3,2	3,3	3,4	3,5
4,1	4,2	4,3	4,4	4,5

we can refer to any box in our table by quoting the pair of numbers contained in the box. You will see that the first of these refers to the row in which the box lies and the second to the column in which it is. For example, the last element in the second row may be referred to as 2,5.

As with lists, we refer to an element of a table by using subscripts, e.g. A(2,5), or by using variable subscripts such as A(I,J). By allowing I and J to vary systematically we can read values into the elements of a table, scan part or all of the table, manipulate the elements and print values as desired.

Tables need dimension statements. These require two subscripts and any reference to an element of a table requires two subscripts. It is meaningless to write

```
10 DIM A(5,6)
20 LET A(4) = 0
```

In sections 8–10 (pages 84–88 of Book 3a), we build up our technique for reading data into a table row by row. This is done in the same way as we introduced loops within loops at the end of Chapter 8 of Book 3a.

When reading data into a table we have to determine beforehand if it is to be read row by row or column by column. The former is the more usual way and for most problems is adequate. We do show, however, at the end of section 10 how data can be read column by column when necessary. Similarly, in section 11 (page 88 of Book 3a) we need to do calculations on columns of a table and it often happens that both row by row and column by column accesses are required in the same program.

Some guidance can be obtained from the program statements of a double loop to see whether calculations are taking place row by row or column by column.

Consider the statements

```
100 FOR I = 1 TO 3
110 FOR J = 1 TO 4
120 PRINT D(I,J)
130 NEXT J
140 NEXT I
```

The inner loop is the one which is executed more quickly (we go round J four times for each increment of I). Therefore the subscript J changes more frequently. In our example J is the second subscript and therefore refers to the *column* in which $D(I,J)$ is counted. Hence, whilst I remains fixed at a given value, J ranges from 1 to 4. That is, we go along the (I)th row, so that printing is row by row.

If, on the other hand, we write

```
200 FOR J = 1 TO 4
210 FOR I = 1 TO 3
220 PRINT D(I,J)
230 NEXT I
240 NEXT J
```

the inner loop refers to I, which is the first subscript so that we are accessing the table column by column.

An alternative way to write the above is to change around the letters I and J. We get:

```
300 FOR I = 1 TO 4
310 FOR J = 1 TO 3
320 PRINT D(J,I)
330 NEXT J
340 NEXT I
```

The DIM statement defining the table D is

```
10 DIM D(3,4)
```

For each of the three examples quoted it will be noticed that the values of the variables I and J lie within the dimensions given. For example, in line 300 I goes between 1 and 4. This corresponds to the second subscript in $D(J,I)$, i.e. $D(3,4)$. The statements

```
10 DIM D(3,4)
400 FOR I = 1 TO 3
410 FOR J = 1 TO 4
420 PRINT D(J,I)
430 NEXT J
440 NEXT I
```

are wrong therefore, since J takes a value 4 which is greater than the corresponding value in the dimension statement.

6 Drawing a histogram

If we make a survey of a group of people and record for each person the month of the year in which they were born, we can draw a histogram to show how many people were born in each month. In order to do this we first read the data, counting up the number of births for each month. This can be done quite simply by using a list M with twelve elements, each one representing a month.

If we write

```
50 READ A
70 LET M(A) = M(A)+1
```

this adds 1 to the count being kept for the (A)th month. For example, if a person is born in July, A=7 and line 70 adds 1 to the count in M(7).

The statements

```
10 DIM M(12)
20 FOR I = 1 TO 12
30 LET M(I) = 0
40 NEXT I
50 READ A
60 IF A<0 THEN 90
70 LET M(A) = M(A)+1
80 GOTO 50
90 . . . .
```

read in all the data (terminated by a negative number).

We draw the histogram by printing out a row of asterisks equal in length to the values in each element of the array. This can be done with the statements:

```
110 FOR I = 1 TO M(A)
120 PRINT "*";
130 NEXT I
```

In order to do this for all elements of the array we enclose these statements in a second loop and, with a few embellishments to provide a caption, numbers for the rows and spacing for clarity, we get the program shown overleaf.

```
10 DIM M(12)
20 FOR I = 1 TO 12
30 LET M(I) = 0
40 NEXT I
50 READ A
60 IF A<0 THEN 90
70 LET M(A) = M(A)+1
80 GOTO 50
90 FOR A = 1 TO 12
100 PRINT
101 IF A>9 THEN 105
102 PRINT A;"      ";
103 GOTO 110
105 PRINT A;"      ";
110 FOR I = 1 TO M(A)
120 PRINT "*";
130 NEXT I
140 NEXT A
150 PRINT
160 PRINT
170 PRINT "HISTOGRAM OF NUMBERS OF BIRTHDAYS"
180 PRINT "PER MONTH IN A SAMPLE POPULATION"
200 REM THE DATA WHICH FOLLOWS, CONSISTING
201 REM OF THE MONTH OF BIRTH OF MEMBERS
202 REM OF THE SAMPLE POPULATION ENDING
203 REM WITH -1 GIVES THE HISTOGRAM
204 REM ILLUSTRATED.

245 DATA 1,2,3,4,5,6,7,8,9,1,3,5,7,9,2,4,6,8
246 DATA 10,10,10,10,10,3,3,3,3,3,3,3,3,3,4
247 DATA 4,4,5,5,5,5,6,6,6,11,11,11,11,12,12
248 DATA 12,12,11,3,5,4,7,7,7,8,8,8,9,10,-1
250 END
```

Note the use of the empty PRINT statement in line 100 to give an extra new line. A specimen of the output from this program follows.

```
 1    **
 2    **
 3    ************
 4    ******
 5    *******
 6    *****
 7    *****
 8    *****
 9    ***
10    ******
11    *****
12    ****
```

HISTOGRAM OF NUMBERS OF BIRTHDAYS
PER MONTH IN A SAMPLE POPULATION

A more general program for drawing histograms may be written quite easily, although some adjustments may need to be made if the number of asterisks is likely to run off the edge of the page.

7 Additional exercises

1. Write a program which reads 40 values into a list, calculates their mean and prints out any values greater than twice the mean. If no such values occur, the program should print a message to this effect.
2. Write a program which reads 20 numbers into a list A, puts the squares of these numbers into corresponding positions in a list B and puts the difference between the corresponding elements of B and A into list C. The program should then print the sums of the elements of lists A, B and C.
3. The preceding exercise is intended to give practice in handling lists and loops. It is not necessary, however, to use lists to do the required calculations. Write a program to do the calculations without using lists.
4. Write a program which reads 50 numbers into a list and prints out the position in the list of any number which is negative.
5. Write a program to read 50 numbers into a list, changing the sign of any negative number before storing it in the list. Print the values of the square roots of the elements of the resulting list.
6. Eight judges are judging an ice-skating contest and they award marks for technical ability and artistic interpretation. The marks awarded are calculated by discarding one of the highest marks and one of the lowest from each set of eight, leaving six marks to be averaged in each case. Write a program to do these calculations and print the results.
7. In a competition, competitors have to put into order eight features (numbered 1 to 8) of a car which they think contribute most to its safety. In the opinion of the judges, the correct order should be 4, 1, 8, 7, 5, 2, 6, 3. Each competitor is given a competitor's number which he writes in front of his choice of order of the eight numbers. Write a program which first reads into a list the judges' ordering of the numbers and then reads in turn sets of competitors' attempts, each attempt being preceded by the competitor's number. The program should compare the competitor's attempt with the judges' decision. If they agree, the competitor's number is to be printed. If they

do not agree, the comparison should be abandoned as soon as a discrepancy is found and the next set of data read. The data are terminated by reading a negative value for the competitor's number.

8. A class, which may have up to 40 students in it, sits five examinations. The five results for each student are read in turn into the computer and are entered into a table. Write a program to accomplish this when the number (N) of students in the class is first read as data. Complete the program by finding the highest mark scored for each subject and storing these marks in a list before printing them out.

9. Twenty people are asked to judge the qualities of a new chocolate wafer biscuit. They have to give a mark on a scale of one to five for each of the following properties— crispness, texture, thickness of chocolate, flavour of the filling. A mark of five indicates that the person liked this property very much, whilst a mark of one indicates a dislike. Write a program to read the 20 sets of four values and to calculate the following:

    (i) the number of marks of three or more scored for each property

    (ii) the average mark scored for each property

    (iii) the number of people who awarded more than three marks to each property

    (iv) the number of people who gave a mark of one in their reply

    (v) the number of people who awarded three marks or more to property 1 (crispness) but did not like the flavour of the filling (property 4) and awarded only one or two marks for this.

10 Additional facilities in BASIC

1 Introduction

There are a number of additional facilities which are not covered in Book 3a but which are available in many versions of BASIC. We describe them in this chapter.

2 The ON statement

This is an extension of the GOTO statement and allows a jump to be made to one of a number of places determined by the value of the variable in the ON statement. The statement is of the form:

```
10 ON X GOTO 7,15,30,45,45,16,12,66
```

Following the GOTO is a list of line numbers. If X has the value N, a jump is made to the line number in the (N)th place in the list. For example,

  if X=3, a jump is made to line 30
  if X=4, a jump is made to line 45
  if X=5, a jump is again made to line 45

If X is less than one or greater than eight (i.e. the number of line numbers given), an 'out of range' error occurs.

Example

We are writing a program to calculate the day of the week corresponding to a given date (day and month) in 1974. We first store in a list A the total number of days which have elapsed before the beginning of each month in the year. After reading the given day and month, we calculate the total number of days which have elapsed until that date by adding to the value of the day the number of days elapsed up to the beginning of that month. This total is divided by seven and the remainder retained. The remainder will be a number in the range 0–6. Since the ON statement works with a list starting at one, we add one to the value of the remainder. We can thus organise a jump to a print statement giving the day of the week. We remember that the 1st of January, 1974 was a Tuesday.

```
10 DIM A(12)
20 FOR I = 1 TO 12
30 READ A(I)
40 NEXT I
45 REM THIS LOOP STORES THE NECESSARY
46 REM ELAPSED DAYS IN LIST A
50 READ D,M
55 IF D<0 THEN 150
60 LET D = D+A(M)
65 REM D NOW EQUALS THE NUMBER OF DAYS
66 REM FROM THE BEGINNING OF THE YEAR
70 LET D = D-INT(D/7)*7+1
80 REM D-INT(D/7)*7 GIVES THE REMAINDER
81 REM WHEN D IS DIVIDED BY 7, WE THEN ADD 1
90 ON D GOTO 100,102,104,106,108,110,112
95 REM NOTICE FIRST OF JANUARY GIVES D=2
100 PRINT "MONDAY"
101 GOTO 50
102 PRINT "TUESDAY"
103 GOTO 50
104 PRINT "WEDNESDAY"
105 GOTO 50
106 PRINT "THURSDAY"
107 GOTO 50
108 PRINT "FRIDAY"
109 GOTO 50
110 PRINT "SATURDAY"
111 GOTO 50
112 PRINT "SUNDAY"
113 GOTO 50
120 DATA 0,31,59,90,120,151,181,212,243
121 DATA 273,304,334
130 DATA<VALUES FOR D & M ENDING WITH -1,-1>
150 END
```

3 The RESTORE facility

We have shown earlier how we normally store data in an array if we wish to use it more than once in a program. It is possible, however, to re-read the information stored in DATA statements if we so desire. This is done by using the RESTORE statement.

We described in Chapter 4, section 3 (page 27) how READ statements obtain the data from DATA statements and in particular how we could imagine a pointer indicating the value which was the next one to be read. The effect of the RESTORE statement is to restore the pointer to the start of the list of data items, so that the next READ statement reads from the start of the first DATA statement again.

Example

The following program calculates and prints the deviations from the mean of a set of positive numbers terminated by −1.

```
10 LET S = 0
20 LET N = 0
30 READ A
40 IF A<0 THEN 80
50 LET S = S+A
60 LET N = N+1
70 GOTO 30
80 LET M = S/N
90 RESTORE
100 FOR I = 1 TO N
110 READ A
120 PRINT A-M
130 NEXT I
140 DATA<SET OF POSITIVE NUMBERS
          ENDING WITH -1>
150 END
```

4 The TAB function

This function provides control of tabulation across the page and occurs in PRINT statements. The effect of TAB(N) in a PRINT list is to cause the next character to be output at the (N)th position on the line. Hence the program

```
10 READ A,B,C,D
20 PRINT A;TAB(6);B;TAB(18);C;TAB(36);D
30 DATA 1,2,3,4
40 END
```

would output the four numerical values spaced across the page as shown below:

```
1       2            3                        4
```

If the current position on the line is in excess of the value indicated in the call of the TAB function, the tabulation is ignored. In the example

```
10 PRINT A,B,C;TAB(20);D
```

the TAB(20) is ineffective, since the two commas have already moved the printing of C into the 29th column.

If the value of N exceeds the maximum permitted number of characters on a line, then N is reduced by multiples of this permitted number in order to bring it into range. Thus TAB(147) and TAB(77) are both equivalent to TAB(7), if the maximum number of permitted characters on a line is 70.

Example

We shall illustrate the use of the TAB function by drawing a graph. It must be appreciated that points plotted on a line printer or teleprinter are necessarily rather crude representations of a curve because of the distance between characters on a line and between the lines themselves.

Care must be taken to see that the scale chosen for the graph is appropriate to the size of paper in use and it must be remembered that paper cannot be wound back on the output device, so that the highest value of the y-coordinate must be printed first. This may necessitate storing results in a list or table and sorting them before printing commences.

In this example we draw the graph of $y=x^2$ for values of $x=0$ to $x=5$. Since the value of y decreases with x we write a loop allowing y to decrease from 25 to 1 in steps of 1 and we calculate the appropriate value of x for each value of y.

The scale of x is chosen to cover 50 character positions along the line. This means that we need to calculate the value of x to one decimal place. To find this value we write:

```
20 LET X = INT( 10*SQR(Y)+0.5)
```

In this statement we have calculated the function $x=\sqrt{y}$ and multiplied by a scaling factor of 10. The nearest integer to this value is then calculated by adding 0·5 and taking the integer part. (See Chapter 3, section 11, page 22.)

In the program below, lines 40 or 60 print an asterisk at the appropriate point of the line. We have allowed for the printing of values of the ordinate y in line 40 and a plus ($+$) sign is used to draw the y-axis. Thus the whole graph is displaced five places to the right. Lines 110 to 231 are concerned with drawing and marking the x-axis and adding a caption to the graph.

The complete program for drawing the graph is:

```
10 FOR Y = 25 TO 1 STEP -1
20 LET X = INT( 10*SQR(Y)+0.5)
30 IF INT(Y/5)*5<>Y THEN 60
40 PRINT Y;TAB(5);"+";TAB(X+5);"*"
50 GOTO 100
60 PRINT TAB(5);"+";TAB(X+5);"*"
100 NEXT Y
110 LET Y = 0
120 PRINT Y;TAB(5);
130 FOR I = 1 TO 51
140 PRINT "+";
150 NEXT I
160 PRINT
170 PRINT TAB(4)
180 FOR I = 0 TO 5
190 PRINT TAB(10*I+4);I;
200 NEXT I
210 PRINT
220 PRINT
230 PRINT TAB(15);
231 PRINT "GRAPH OF Y = X*X FOR X=0 TO X=5"
240 END
```

The output from this program produced on a teleprinter is shown below.

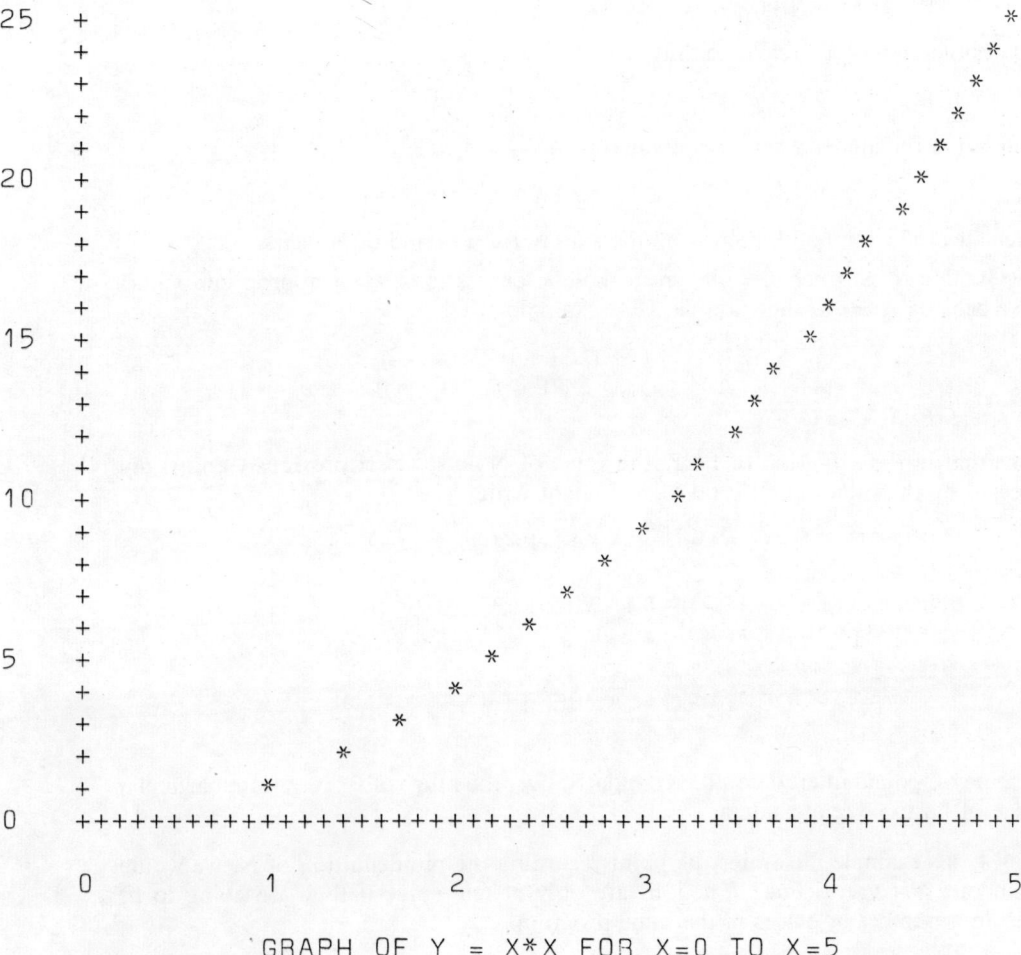

GRAPH OF Y = X*X FOR X=0 TO X=5

5 User-defined functions

We have seen that some frequently used functions (e.g. SQR(X), ABS(X), etc.) are provided by the BASIC system and that these functions may be used in the same way as variables. It is useful for a user to be able to define similar functions for special purposes and this can easily be done. The definition is made in the program and is only valid within it. We shall limit ourselves to describing functions with one variable which can be defined on one line, although some BASIC systems allow more complex multi-line definitions. The definition is of the form

```
10 DEF FNZ(X) = . . . .
```

where the right-hand side of the statement consists of the arithmetic expression to be evaluated. The letters DEF FN are standard but the following letter may be any one from the alphabet, thus allowing a number of functions to be defined in the same program.

69

```
10 DEF FNA(X) = 3.142*X*X
```

defines the area of a circle of radius X.

```
20 DEF FNR(X) = X-INT(X/4)*4
```

defines the remainder when X is divided by 4.

```
30 DEF FNZ(X) = (1-X↑(N+1))/(1-X)-X
```

calculates the compound interest on the sum X for a period of N years.

The functions can then be used in arithmetic expressions when appropriate values have been assigned to the variables. For example:

```
50 LET W = FNA(X)+FNA(Y)+FNA(Z)
60 ON 1+FNR(A) GOTO 10,20,30,40
70 PRINT FNZ(P)
```

Note that in the definition of FNZ, the value of N must be set previously and is not affected by the value which P takes. We might write

```
10 DEF FNZ(X) = (1-X↑(N+1))/(1-X)-X
20 READ N
30 FOR P = 1000 TO 5000 STEP 100
40 PRINT FNZ(P)
50 NEXT P
60 DATA<REQUIRED VALUE OF N>
70 END
```

so that compound interest could be tabulated over the range of P given for a particular value of N, to be read as data.

Whilst this example illustrates the point regarding the pre-definition of N, we would point out that user-defined functions are only of real value if they are going to be used in a number of places in the same program.

6 Subroutines

Sometimes it is necessary to repeat a set of instructions several times at different places in the same program. Instead of writing out these statements each time, we can write them once as a *subroutine* and place this at the end of the program. At the appropriate place in the program a jump can be made to this subroutine by using a GOSUB statement. When the statements of the subroutine have been carried out, the main program continues at the statement following the one from which the jump was made.

Obviously it is necessary to have some method of returning to the correct place in the program. This is effected by putting a RETURN instruction after the last statement in the subroutine. When a GOSUB statement is executed, the line number of the following statement is stored and the RETURN statement uses this to go back to the main program. We illustrate this below, where three jumps are made to a subroutine whose line numbering begins with 1000.

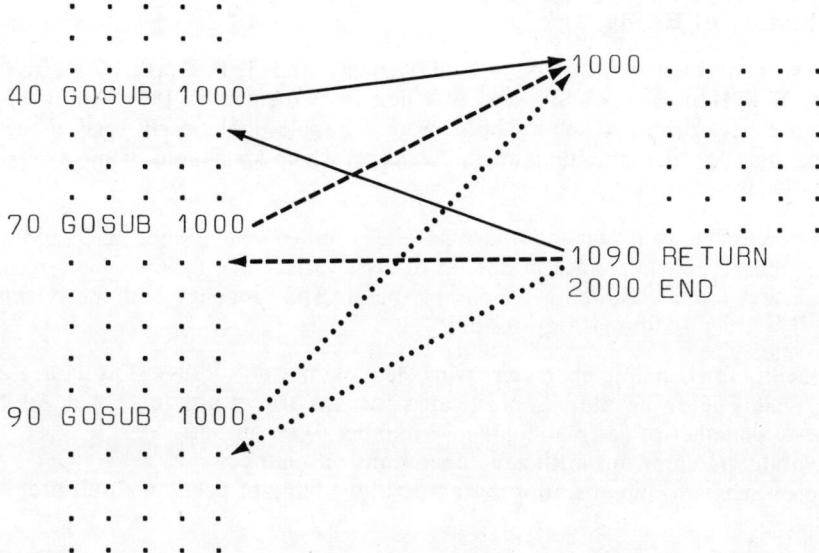

There can, of course, be more than one subroutine in a program, each one being terminated by a RETURN statement. Exits from subroutines must be by means of a RETURN statement only and not by other jumps, otherwise correct sequencing is lost. It is also possible to have a GOSUB statement within a subroutine, thus allowing a jump to a further subroutine.

There can be a number of RETURN statements in the same routine but only one of these will be executed for any entry into the routine. In the example below, four numbers are read in and various additions and subtractions of these numbers are carried out. After each calculation a jump is made to a subroutine to test whether the result is negative or non-negative. In the subroutine, the RETURN statement of line 140 is used to get back to the main program when the result is negative, otherwise the return is by means of line 120.

```
10  READ A,B,C,D
20  LET X = A-B-C-D
30  GOSUB 100
40  LET X = A+B-C-D
50  GOSUB 100
60  LET X = A+B+C-D
70  GOSUB 100
80  LET X = A+B+C+D
90  GOSUB 100
95  GOTO 200
100 IF X<0 THEN 130
110 PRINT "NOT NEGATIVE"
120 RETURN
130 PRINT "NEGATIVE"
140 RETURN
150 DATA<VALUES OF A,B,C,D>
200 END
```

7 The history of BASIC

BASIC was invented by Professors J G Kemeny and T E Kurtz of Dartmouth College, New Hampshire, USA, and was first implemented in 1964. Many of the features we have discussed in this book were available in the early versions of the language and they form the fundamental concepts which are shared by most versions of BASIC now available.

Besides developments at Dartmouth, other establishments have since made additions to the language and implementations on a large variety of machines have resulted in the production of different versions of the BASIC language and the operating system. The chief additional features are:

(i) the facility for handling character strings (e.g. names or addresses) as data
(ii) the facility allowing more sophisticated formats for results (e.g. being able to describe the number of decimal digits of a number to be output)
(iii) the ability to carry out arithmetic operations on matrices
(iv) improvements to the operating system to allow filing of programs, sub-programs and data.

8 A standard BASIC

An attempt to produce a universally accepted standard for the BASIC programming system has recently been published under the auspices of the National Computing Centre Limited. The book, *Specification for Standard Basic**, defines the language and its elements. This is not suitable for anyone learning BASIC or for anyone inexperienced in computing. It is intended to be a reference manual for people wishing to implement BASIC on a computer, or to act as a definitive text when clarification on some obscure point is required. Standardisation of the various forms of BASIC is desirable, however, and such a specification is required before this can be done.

9 Additional exercises

1. Use the ON statement to modify the example (Chapter 9, section 6, page 61) in which a histogram is drawn, so that the abbreviations JAN, FEB, MAR, . . ., DEC appear at the left-hand side of the output in place of the numbers 1, 2, 3, . . ., 12 shown in the illustration on page 63.
2. Use the TAB function in a program which prints out the numbers 123, 234, . . ., 789 in the form shown below:

```
123
 234
  345
   456
    567
     678
      789
```

3. A manufacturer sells an article costing £A, where the value of A is input as data. To one class of customer he has to charge 10% VAT on the selling price, to a second class of customer he has to make the same charges but he can give a 5% discount on

---

* '*Specification for Standard Basic*', *G M Bull, W Freeman and S J Garland. Published by NCC Publications, 1973.*

the selling price. It is also possible that he can recover import duty amounting to 3% of the selling price. Write a program which prints the total cost to the first class of customer and which, for the second class of customer, prints

(i) the total cost including VAT

(ii) the value calculated in (i) but with the discount applied

(iii) the value calculated in (ii) but with the element of import duty removed.

If A contains a decimal fraction, the function $INT(100*A+0.5)/100$ calculates the value of A correct to two decimal places (e.g. if $A=3.14159$, then $INT(100*A+0.5)/100=3.14$). Use this function in the program, so that the answers are correct to the nearest penny.

4. In Chapter 4 of Book 3a, there are a number of illustrations of computer output. These were produced by writing a BASIC program which gave all the output required. For the printer's convenience it was necessary to separate each illustration by ten lines of blank paper. Write a program which would produce this output for the printer.

5. A programmer having written a long BASIC program discovers that he needs to insert about 20 new statements between, say, lines 40 and 50. How could he make use of the GOSUB facility to introduce these statements at the appropriate place without needing to renumber all the subsequent statements of his program?

11 An interactive example

1 Introduction

In this chapter we show the various stages of analysing a problem, producing a flow chart and writing the program. We choose as our example the game of snakes and ladders and write a program so that the game can be played at a computer terminal.

The program incorporates many of the ideas which have been put forward in the previous chapters. In particular we use subroutines to simulate the throwing of the die and to calculate the position on the board. The random number generator is used to calculate the value of the throw. A list keeps values representing positions on the board and the READ statement is used to input these values.

New features are the use of the INPUT statement when the user is required to type in a value, and the prompting messages printed out by the program to ask the player to make a move. The program is thus truly interactive since the game is played following a series of instructions given by the computer.

2 Definition of the problem

In any problem we must be certain about our objectives, otherwise we may not achieve them. In the case of snakes and ladders, for instance, we should be sure of how the game is played and of the rules which are to be obeyed. There are in fact many variations of the rules and when writing a description of a program such as this, the rules should be stated so that the user knows them. We define them as follows, using a board with 25 squares as an illustration.

The game is played on a board with 25 numbered squares. Snakes and ladders are drawn on the board connecting various squares. There are two players, each of whom has a counter. Moves are determined by the throw of a die.

Initially each player throws the die. The player with the higher throw starts. (If the throws are equal, the process is repeated.) On commencing the game the player moves his counter along the board over the number of squares equal to the value on

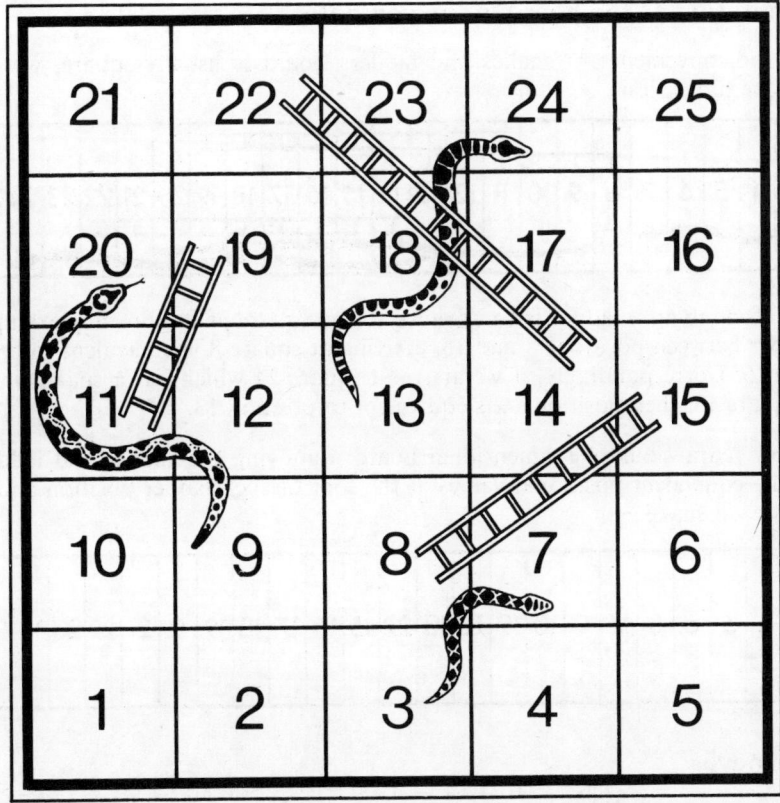

the die. Each player takes it in turn to throw. For example, if Player 1 throws a 4, his counter is moved to square 4; if Player 2 then throws a 2, his counter is moved to square 2. In the next throw, Player 1 throws a 5 and his counter goes to square 9 (4+5), and so on.

There is only one exception to this alternate throwing. If a player throws a 6, he moves his counter six places and takes another throw.

If at the end of a player's move the counter rests on the foot of a ladder, he moves his counter to the top of the ladder. If at the end of a move the counter rests on the head of a snake, the player moves his counter to the square containing the snake's tail. If a player lands at the bottom of a ladder or at the head of a snake after throwing a 6, he must go up or down before making his next move.

As the player approaches square 25, the value on the die may be greater than the number of squares needed to reach 25. For example, if the player is on square 23 and he throws a 4, he would 'go beyond' 25. In this case he does not move his counter but remains where he is (unless he has thrown a 6 and is entitled to another throw). The winner of the game is the player who first arrives at square 25.

Writing the specifications for the game has taken quite a few lines of text but if detailed specifications are not drawn up it is impossible to go into the details of designing and writing the program to carry out the game.

3 Representation of the board in the computer

Although, for convenience, a snakes and ladders board is usually square, we can draw it in one dimension:

The effect of climbing a ladder is to advance to the square at its top. For example, with a ladder between positions 8 and 15, arriving at square 8 is equivalent to being in position 15. Correspondingly, if we arrive at square 24 which has a snake whose tail is in square 13, then position 24 is equivalent to position 13.

We can now redraw our one-dimensional board, removing the snakes and ladders and inserting equivalent positional values at the foot of each ladder position and at the head of each snake.

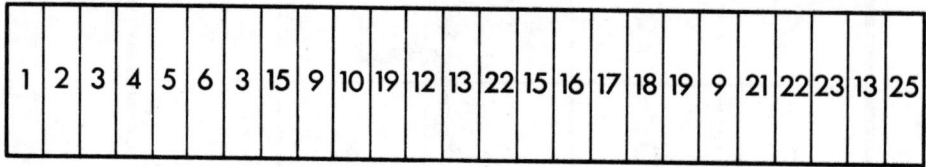

4 Making moves

If we now start a game by throwing a 5, we can check that we move to the fifth position because the value 5 is in the fifth square. In our next throw, if we throw a 3, we add 3 to 5. In the eighth square is the value 15, so the result is the equivalent of being on square 15. A throw now of 5 takes us to square 20. Since the value in square 20 is 9, we 'return' to square 9.

Translating this into computer terms we keep, in S, our position on the board. The values in the twenty-five squares are kept in a list B. From this list we see, for instance, that B(5) contains the value 5, B(8) contains the value 15 and B(20) the value 9. Initially S = 0 (i.e. off the board). A throw of 5 makes S = 5. We now look at B(5) to find the value stored there, since this is the new position on the board.

This is equivalent to saying

```
630 LET S = B(S)
```

Since B(5) = 5, S retains the value 5. If 3 is now thrown this is added to 5. Hence S = 8, B(8) = 15 and the statement

```
630 LET S = B(S)
```

gives S the value 15 (equivalent to 'move to 15').

5 A subroutine to find the position on the board

We base the subroutine on the discussion in the previous section, elaborating it slightly by printing out the position on the board after the throw, together with a remark if we go up a ladder or down a snake. We also take care of the case where we may exceed the value 25.

The flow chart for the subroutine is:

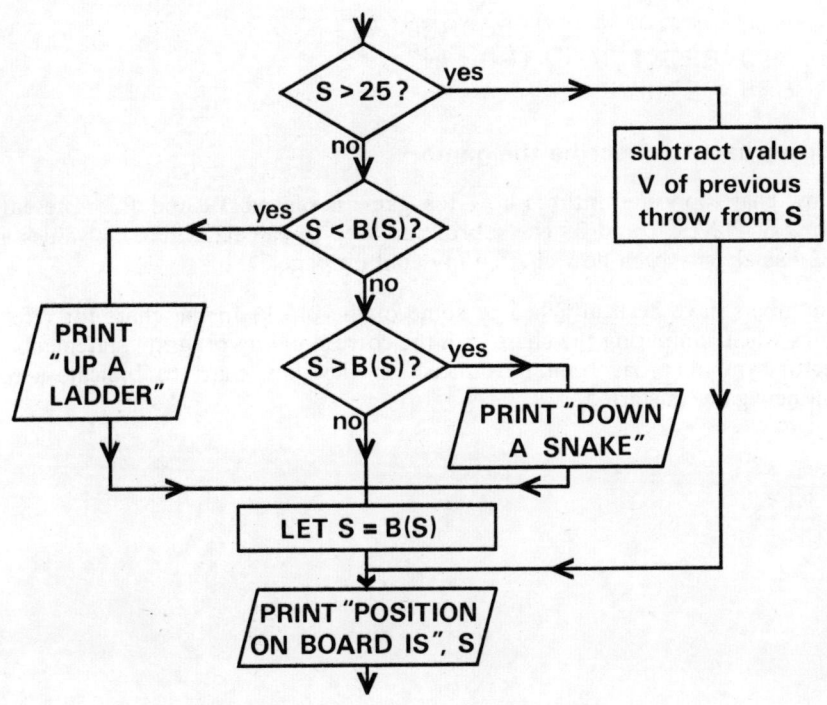

and the corresponding subroutine is:

```
600 IF S>25 THEN 660
610 IF S<B(S) THEN 680
620 IF S>B(S) THEN 700
630 LET S = B(S)
640 PRINT "POSITION ON THE BOARD IS":S
650 GOTO 720
660 LET S = S-V
670 GOTO 640
680 PRINT "UP A LADDER"
690 GOTO 630
700 PRINT "DOWN A SNAKE"
710 GOTO 630
720 RETURN
```

6 A subroutine for throwing the die

We use the random number generator to obtain one of the values 1 to 6 and to print the value thrown. To add a little realism to the game, we make each player type a number to indicate that he is making a throw. This number is not used in the program, it merely serves to hold up the action whilst the previous result is examined. The subroutine is:

```
500 INPUT A
510 LET V = INT(6*RND(A)+1)
520 PRINT V;" THROWN"
530 RETURN
```

7 A flow chart to describe the game

The flow chart opposite outlines how the game is played. P1 and P2 represent the positions of Players 1 and 2. The subroutine used to calculate the new values at P1 and P2 has already been flow charted in detail on page 77.

Line numbers have been attached to some of the blocks in the chart for reference purposes when comparing the chart with the corresponding program statements. The connector symbol ① has been introduced on the flow chart to indicate a return when a new game is started.

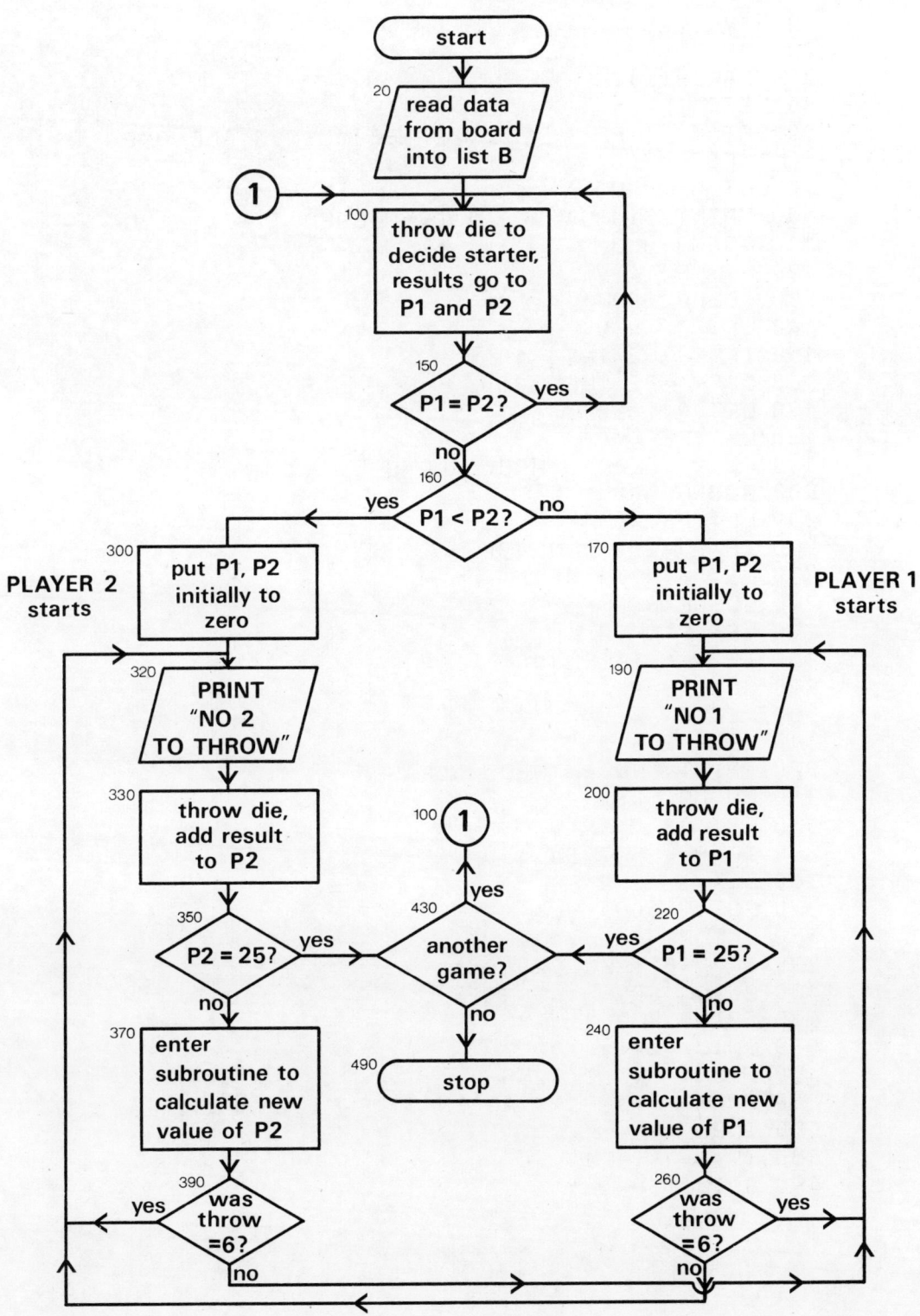

```
10 DIM B(25)
20 FOR I = 1 TO 25
30 READ B(I)
40 NEXT I
50 PRINT "TYPE ANY NUMBER BETWEEN 1 AND 999"
60 INPUT A
70 LET S = RND(A)
100 PRINT "THROW TO START,HIGHER THROW WINS"
110 GOSUB 500
120 LET P1 = V
130 GOSUB 500
140 LET P2 = V
150 IF P1=P2 THEN 110
160 IF P1<P2 THEN 300
170 LET P1 = 0
180 LET P2 = 0
190 PRINT "NO 1 THROW PLEASE"
200 GOSUB 500
210 LET P1 = P1+V
220 IF P1=25 THEN 430
230 LET S = P1
240 GOSUB 600
250 LET P1 = S
260 IF V=6 THEN 190
270 GOTO 320
300 LET P1 = 0
310 LET P2 = 0
320 PRINT "NO 2 THROW PLEASE"
330 GOSUB 500
340 LET P2 = P2+V
350 IF P2=25 THEN 450
360 LET S = P2
370 GOSUB 600
380 LET P2 = S
390 IF V=6 THEN 320
400 GOTO 190
430 PRINT "NO 1 WINS"
440 GOTO 460
450 PRINT "NO 2 WINS"
460 PRINT "TO PLAY AGAIN TYPE 1, OTHERWISE 0"
470 INPUT A
480 IF A=1 THEN 100
490 GOTO 830
```

```
500 INPUT A
510 LET V = INT(6*RND(A)+1)
520 PRINT V;"THROWN"
530 RETURN
600 IF S>25 THEN 660
610 IF S<B(S) THEN 680
620 IF S>B(S) THEN 700
630 LET S = B(S)
640 PRINT "POSITION ON THE BOARD IS";S
650 GOTO 720
660 LET S = S-V
670 GOTO 640
680 PRINT "UP A LADDER"
690 GOTO 630
700 PRINT "DOWN A SNAKE"
710 GOTO 630
720 RETURN
800 DATA 1,2,3,4,5,6,3,15,9,10
810 DATA 19,12,13,22,15,16,17,18
820 DATA 19,9,21,22,23,13,25
830 END
```

8 The main program

This is in several parts.

Lines 10–70 set up the initial information, the values on the board being read from data statements 800–820.

Lines 50–70 allow for the possibility that the random number generator can be 'started' at different values.

Lines 100–160 determine who starts. Notice that if both players throw the same value, they try again. Also notice that the 'throwing' subroutine is used twice here. The variables P1 and P2 are used to keep the positions of Players 1 and 2.

Lines 170 and 180 set up the initial conditions with both players off the board.

Lines 190–270 correspond to the first player's throw. Access is made to both sub-routines, and allowance is made for another turn if a 6 is thrown. A check is also made to see if the end of the board is reached. Notice that we have to transfer the value of P1 to S in the subroutine and retrieve it afterwards.

Lines 300–400 are the second player's throw. Here P2 goes to S in the subroutine.

Lines 430–490 are the concluding stages. The STOP statement could have been used as an alternative in line 490 since this is the logical end of the program. If line 490 were omitted, the program instead of coming to an end would pass into the sub-routines and run amok.

9 Additional exercises

1. Modify the program so that a player who has thrown a 6 does not go up a ladder or down a snake before his next throw.
2. Modify the program so that a player cannot start until he has thrown a 6. The value of his next throw then determines his first position on the board.
3. Modify the program so that if a player's new position is already occupied by his opponent the move is nullified.

Solutions to exercises
in Book 3a and Teachers' Book 3a

Where relevant, the solutions have been written as complete programs with appropriate data. When testing the data, other sets of data may also be required to ensure that all possibilities are covered. In one or two instances, where a large amount of data is required, some DATA statements have been omitted. This is indicated by a row of dots.

For the convenience of the printer it was necessary to limit the length of program lines to no more than 45 characters. This has caused some modifications to programs which would not normally be required. For instance, PRINT statements are frequently shared between two lines, using the semi-colon facility so that the results when output will remain on one line. The solution to Exercise 1, Chapter 10, Teachers' Book 3a has had to be manipulated so that the ON statement (line 101) contains small values for the line numbers to allow the instruction to fit on one line. A more natural way to write the program would have been to put the PRINT statements later in the program but this, of course, would have entailed three-digit line numbers.

Solutions to the exercises are given chapter by chapter, the solutions to the exercises in Book 3a preceding those for the Teachers' Book.

Please note that in the answers section the computer program segments have been reproduced at half their original size. All other computer program segments in this book and in Book 3a are reproduced at their correct size.

Chapter 2

Book 3a

Exercise 1, question 1

```
10 READ R,H,T
20 LET W = R*H+T
30 PRINT W
40 DATA 50,12,70
50 END
```

Exercise 1, question 2

```
10 READ N,W
20 LET T = N*W
30 PRINT T
40 DATA 7,4
50 END
```

Teachers' Book 3a

Exercise 1

```
10 READ A,N
20 LET C = A*N
30 PRINT C
40 DATA 17,8
50 END
```

Exercise 2

```
10 READ T,W
20 LET L = W-T
30 PRINT L
40 DATA 5.4,9.3
50 END
```

Exercise 3

```
10 READ A,B,C
20 LET T = A+B+C
30 PRINT A,B,C,T
40 DATA 3,4,5
50 END
```

Chapter 3

Book 3a

Exercise 1

T, C1, C2, I1, A8

Exercise 2, question 1

E has been used in an expression (line 30) without having had a value assigned to it.

Exercise 2, question 2

We cannot write an expression on the left-hand side of an assignment statement (line 30), nor has W been given a value.

Exercise 3

$A+B-C, A*B*C, A*B-C, A/B + C*D, C+D/E, A*B/C, A+B/C, X*Y*A$

Exercise 4

line 10   A10 not allowed
line 20   2B not allowed
line 30   — in place of =
line 40   no LET in the statement
line 50   A+B on left-hand side of =
line 60   3A, 6B not allowed
line 70   LEF in place of LET
line 80   6 not allowed after LET

Exercise 5

$$X\uparrow2 + Y\uparrow2, \ 3\cdot14*R\uparrow2$$

Exercise 6, question 1

    (i) $24/4/2 = 6/2 = 3$

    (ii) $24/4*3 = 6*3 = 18$

    (iii) $12 + 4*3 = 12+12 = 24$

    (iv) $15 + 10/5 = 15 + 2 = 17$

    (v) $10 + 3\uparrow2 = 10 + 9 = 19$

    (vi) $5*3 + 4*7 = 15 + 4*7 = 15 + 28 = 43$

    (vii) $8\uparrow2*2 = 64*2 = 128$

    (viii) $3*2\uparrow3+2 = 3*8+2 = 24+2 = 26$

    (ix) $2\uparrow3 - 3*2\uparrow2 + 6 = 8 - 3*2\uparrow2 + 6 = 8 - 3*4+6 = 8 - 12 + 6 = -4 + 6 = 2$

    (x) $30/3*5 = 10*5 = 50$

Exercise 6, question 2

    72, 9, 7·5408, 8·04352

Exercise 7, question 1

    (i) $(24/4)/2 = 6/2 = 3$

    (ii) $24/(4/2) = 24/2 = 12$

    (iii) $24/4/2 = 6/2 = 3$

    (iv) $24/4*3 = 6*3 = 18$

    (v) $(24/4)*3 = 6*3 = 18$

    (vi) $24/(4*3) = 24/12 = 2$

    (vii) $12 + 4*3 = 12 + 12 = 24$

    (viii) $12 + (4*3) = 12 + 12 = 24$

    (ix) $(12 + 4)*3 = 16*3 = 48$

    (x) $(2 + 8)/(4 + 1) = 10/(4 + 1) = 10/5 = 2$

    (xi) $(3 + 2)\uparrow2 = 5\uparrow2 = 25$

    (xii) $(5 - 3)\uparrow3 = 2\uparrow3 = 8$

    (xiii) $((2+8)/2)\uparrow2 = (10/2)\uparrow2 + 5\uparrow2 = 25$

    (xiv) $100/(2+3)/4 = 100/5/4 = 20/4 = 5$

    (xv) $(2*2 + 3)*2\uparrow5 = (4 + 3)*2\uparrow5 = 7*2\uparrow5 = 7*32 = 224$

    (xvi) $((2*2 + 3)*2 + 5)*2 + 6 = ((4 + 3)*2 + 5)*2 + 6 =$
$(7*2 + 5)*2 + 6 = (14 + 5)*2+6 = 19*2 + 6 = 38 + 6 = 44$

Exercise 7, question 2

    (i)

```
20 LET M = (A+B+C+D+E+F+G)/7
```

    (ii)

```
20 LET W = H*R+T
```

    (iii)

```
20 LET V = 3.142*R↑2*H
```

    (iv)

```
20 LET C = W+5*T
```

Exercise 8

    (i)

```
10 READ A,B,C,D,E,F,G
20 LET M = (A+B+C+D+E+F+G)/7
30 PRINT M
40 DATA 3,4,5,2,1,8,6
50 END
```

    (ii)

```
10 READ H,R,T
20 LET W = H*R+T
30 PRINT W
40 DATA 50,12,75
50 END
```

    (iii)

```
10 READ R,H
20 LET V = 3.142*R↑2*H
30 PRINT V
40 DATA 3,4
50 END
```

(iv)
```
10 READ W,T
20 LET C = W+5*T
30 PRINT C
40 DATA 4.5,1.2
50 END
```

Exercise 9

```
10 READ A
20 LET R = SQR(A/3.142)
30 PRINT R
40 DATA 10
50 END
```

Exercise 10
$$D = 2, E = 14, F = 7$$

Teachers' Book 3a
Exercise 1
(a) `10 LET A = P+Q+R`

(b) `10 LET B = 2*A`

(c) `10 LET C = 3*A+2*B`

(d) `10 LET Z = X*Y+5`

(e) `10 LET P = P+Q`

Exercise 2
(a) `10 LET D = A/(B+C)`

(b) `10 LET M = (X+Y+Z+W)/4`

(c) `10 LET A = 2*(B+C)+6`

Exercise 3

	line no.	A	B	C	D
(a)	10	2	1	?	?
	20	2	1	1	?
	30	2	1	1	−3
	40	2	1	−5	−3
	50	2	−10	−5	−3
	60	−2·5	−10	−5	−3
(b)	10	1	2	?	?
	20	1	2	0·5	?
	30	1	2	0·5	1
	40	1	2	0·333	1
	50	1	2	1·333	1
	60	1	2	1·333	9·333
(c)	10	?	?	2	?
	20	1	?	2	?
	30	1	0·333	2	?
	40	1	0·333	2	3
	50	1	0·333	0	3
	60	1	0·333	0	0
(d)	10	3	4	?	?
	20	3	4	7	?
	30	3	4	7	5

Exercise 4

```
10 READ M,N
20 LET P = 9*M-3*N
30 PRINT P
40 DATA 25,21
50 END
```

Exercise 5

```
10 READ F,S
20 LET E = (F-S)*4
30 PRINT E
40 DATA 13245,13114
50 END
```

Exercise 6

```
10 READ A,B,C
20 LET X = 4*A
30 LET Y = 0.85*B
40 LET Z = 0.40*C
50 LET W = X+Y+Z
60 PRINT X,Y,Z,W
70 END
```

Exercise 7

```
10 READ R
20 LET A = 0.858*R↑2
30 REM AREA IS 4*R↑2-3.142*R↑2
40 PRINT A
50 DATA 3
60 END
```

Exercise 8

```
10 READ M,N,P
20 LET P = 1.70*M+1.40*N+1.80*P
30 PRINT P
40 DATA 12,14,3
50 END
```

Exercise 9

```
20 LET S = INT(6*RND(X)+1)+INT(6*RND(X)+1)
30 REM NOTE THAT THIS STATEMENT IS NOT SAME
31 REM AS 2*INT(6*RND(X)+1), SINCE THE
32 REM FUNCTION RND IS CALLED TWICE IN
33 REM LINE 20. I.E. TWO SHAKES OF THE DIE.
40 PRINT S
70 END
```

Exercise 10

```
10 READ A,B,C,D,E
20 LET A1 = ABS(A)+ABS(B)+ABS(C)+ABS(D)+ABS(E)
30 LET A2 = ABS(A+B+C+D+E)
40 PRINT A1,A2
50 DATA 1,-2,3,-4,5
60 END
```

Exercise 11

(a)
```
10 LET W = A+B
20 LET X = 1/W
30 LET Y = W/(1+W)
40 LET Z = A+B/(1+W)
```

(b)
```
5 LET X = SQR(A)
6 LET Y = SQR(B)
10 LET P = X+Y
20 LET Q = X*Y
30 LET R = 1+Q
```

(c)
```
5 LET W1 = 1/H1
6 LET W2 = 1/H2
7 LET W3 = W1+1+W2
10 LET P1 = W1/W3
20 LET P2 = 1/W3
30 LET P3 = W2/W3
```

Chapter 4

Book 3a

Exercise 1, question 1

```
10 PRINT "PRINTING EXERCISE"
20 END
```

Exercise 1, question 2

```
10 PRINT "JOHN SMITH"
20 PRINT "10 NEW STREET"
30 PRINT "NEWTOWN"
40 END
```

Exercise 2

If you put

```
20 PRINT ""THE GABLES""
```

the first two sets of quotation marks would be taken as the opening
and closing signs for printing what lies between them—in this case nothing.
The computer would not expect text to follow immediately and an error
would be indicated.

Teachers' Book 3a

Exercise 1

```
10 READ A,B
20 PRINT "A","B","A+B","SQUARE OF A+B"
30 PRINT A,B,A+B,(A+B)*(A+B)
40 DATA 3,4
50 END
```

Exercise 2

```
10 READ A,B
20 PRINT "A=";A
30 PRINT "B=";B
40 PRINT "A+B=";A+B
50 PRINT "SQUARE OF A+B=";(A+B)*(A+B)
60 DATA 3,4
70 END
```

Exercise 3

```
10 READ Y,M,D1,M1,Y1
20 PRINT "MY AGE IS";Y;" YEARS";M;" MONTHS"
30 PRINT "MY DATE OF BIRTH IS";
31 PRINT D1;"/";M1;"/";Y1
40 DATA 14,3,15,2,60
50 END
```

Chapter 5

Book 3a

Exercise 1, question 1(a)

```
10 READ R
20 LET A = 3.142*R
30 PRINT A
40 DATA 2
50 END
```

Exercise 1, question 1(b)

Insert

```
5 FOR I = 1 TO 10
35 NEXT I
```

and put ten numbers in the DATA statement.

Exercise 1, question 2(a)

```
10 READ L
20 LET P = L*0.12
30 PRINT P,L
40 DATA 5
50 END
```

Exercise 1, question 2(b)

Insert

```
5 FOR I = 1 TO 15
35 NEXT I
```

and put fifteen numbers in DATA statements.

Exercise 1, question 3

```
10 FOR I = 1 TO 6
20 READ R,H
30 LET W = R*H
40 PRINT W
50 NEXT I
60 DATA 50,35,48,37.5,58,36
70 DATA 48,25,50,21,62,41
80 END
```

Exercise 1, question 4

```
10 FOR I = 1 TO 20
20 READ K
30 LET E = K*4
40 PRINT E
50 NEXT I
60 DATA 27,31,14,7,15,26,83,114,23,17
70 DATA 46,15,9,23,28,17,49,86,171,28
80 END
```

Exercise 2

Insert

```
3 READ N
```

and change line 5 to

```
5 FOR I = 1 TO N
```

Exercise 3, question 1

```
10 FOR I = 1 TO 10
20 PRINT SQR(I)
30 NEXT I
40 END
```

Exercise 3, question 2

```
10 PRINT "MILES","KILOMETRES"
20 READ N
30 FOR I = 1 TO N
40 LET K = 1.6*I
50 PRINT I,K
60 NEXT I
70 END
```

Teachers' Book 3a

Exercise 1

```
10 LET S1 = 0
20 LET S2 = 0
30 FOR I = 1 TO 20
40 READ A,B
50 LET S1 = S1+A
60 LET S2 = S2+B
70 NEXT I
80 LET M1 = S1/20
90 LET M2 = S2/20
100 PRINT M1,M2
110 DATA 17,19,47,43,21,25,43,37,36,35
120 DATA 24,36,7,10,14,25,27,28,50,47
130 DATA 33,36,18,17,26,23,45,47,38,36
140 DATA 27,38,16,30,35,24,29,31,18,4
150 END
```

Exercise 2

```
10 LET S1 = 0
20 LET S2 = 0
30 FOR I = 1 TO 15
40 READ A,B
50 LET S1 = S1+A
60 LET S2 = S2+B
70 NEXT I
80 LET M1 = S1/15
90 LET M2 = S2/15
100 PRINT M1,M2
110 DATA 42.3,31.6,43.6,32.5,41.5,33.6
120 DATA 43.0,35.0,39.8,29.7,42.7,31.2
130 DATA 41.5,30.3,43.4,32.6,44.7,34.3
140 DATA 39.7,29.9,41.6,33.7,42.5,34.1
150 DATA 40.7,30.6,41.2,31.3,40.4,30.3
160 END
```

Exercise 3

In the above two solutions, read a value N before line 30, alter line 30 by putting N at the end of the FOR statements and alter lines 80 and 90 by dividing by N.

Exercise 4

(a)
```
10 LET S = 0
20 FOR I = 1 TO 10
30 LET S = S+I
40 NEXT I
50 PRINT S
60 END
```

(b) Read a value of N before line 20 and replace 10 by N in line 20.

Exercise 5

```
10 LET S = 0
20 READ N
30 FOR I = 1 TO N
40 LET S = S+I*I
50 NEXT I
60 PRINT S
70 DATA 50
80 END
```

Exercise 6

```
10 FOR I = 1 TO 12
20 PRINT "12 *";I;" =";12*I
30 NEXT I
40 END
```

Chapter 6

Book 3a

Exercise 1, question 1

    (i)   `10 DIM S(11)`

    (ii)   `10 DIM M(12)`

    (iii) `10 DIM H(18)`

Exercise 1, question 2

    (a) 9, 7, 3, 1

    (b) 2, −3, −1, 2, 9, 0

Exercise 2, question 1

    2, 4, 6, 4, 12, 24, 16

Exercise 2, question 2

    10, 10, 8

Exercise 3

The program adds together in S the value contained in the list A and prints the result, i.e. 17.

Teachers' Book 3a

Exercise 1

```
10 DIM T(8),A(8)
20 FOR I = 1 TO 8
30 READ T(I)
40 NEXT I
50 FOR I = 1 TO 8
60 READ A(I)
70 NEXT I
80 LET S1 = 0
90 LET S2 = 0
100 FOR I = 1 TO 8
110 LET S1 = S1+T(I)
120 LET S2 = S2+A(I)
130 NEXT I
140 PRINT S1/8,S2/8
150 DATA 5.4,5.6,5.6,5.7,5.5,5.6,5.8,5.7
160 DATA 5.5,5.6,5.5,5.4,5.7,5.8,5.6,5.5
170 END
```

Exercise 2

```
10 DIM D(52),S(52)
20 FOR I = 1 TO 52
30 READ D(I),S(I)
40 NEXT I
50 LET S1 = 0
60 LET S2 = 0
70 FOR I = 1 TO 52
80 LET S1 = S1+D(I)
90 LET S2 = S2+S(I)
100 NEXT I
110 PRINT "TOTAL NO OF DELUXE =";S1
120 PRINT "TOTAL NO OF SUPERS =";S2
130 PRINT "AV. NO OF DELUXE =";S1/52
140 PRINT "AV. NO OF SUPERS =";S2/52
145 PRINT
150 PRINT "WEEK","TOTAL SOLD"
160 FOR I = 1 TO 52
170 LET T = D(I)+S(I)
180 PRINT I,T
190 NEXT I
200 PRINT
210 PRINT "TOTAL NO OF CARS SOLD =";S1+S2
220 DATA 5,3,4,2,3,4,0,1,2,3,1,1,5,1,4
230 DATA 2,3,3,6,2,1,4,3,2,1,1,2,3,2,2
240 DATA 3,1,1,2,0,1,1,0,2,2,2,2,1,0,0
250 DATA 0,2,2,1,3,4,2,5,4,3,7,2,1,1,0
260 DATA 2,2,1,3,2,4,4,0,0,0,1,0,0,0,1
270 DATA 0,2,3,1,4,0,0,0,0,0,0,1,2,4,1
280 DATA 3,3,7,2,1,4,2,1,1,0,1,1,1,2
290 END
```

Exercise 3

```
10 DIM P(6)
20 FOR I = 1 TO 6
30 READ P(I)
40 NEXT I
50 LET S = 0
60 FOR I = 1 TO 6
70 READ A
80 LET S = S+A*P(I)
85 REM IN THE LOOP THE NUMBER OF SHIRTS
86 REM REQUIRED IS READ AND MULTIPLIED
87 REM BY THE APPROPRIATE PRICE
90 NEXT I
100 PRINT "COST OF ORDER =";S
110 DATA 1.35,1.40,1.50,1.60,1.73,1.85
120 DATA 3,4,2,1,0,0
130 END
```

Chapter 7

Book 3a

Exercise 1

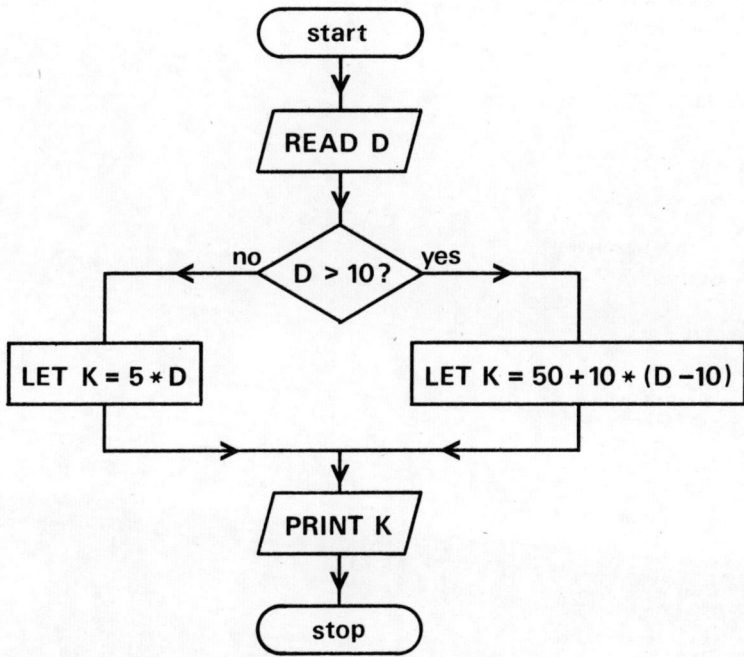

```
10 READ D
20 IF D>10 THEN 50
30 LET K = 5*D
40 GOTO 60
50 LET K = 50+10*(D-10)
60 PRINT K
70 DATA 4
80 END
```

Exercise 2

```
10 IF A<1 THEN 200
10 IF B>A THEN 200
10 IF C>=D THEN 200
10 IF B<>9 THEN 200
10 IF D=0 THEN 200
10 IF T<=60 THEN 200
```

Exercise 3, question 1
  Replace line 30 with

```
30 IF C>5 THEN 50
```

  and delete lines 100-120. Line 80 may also be deleted.

Exercise 3, question 2

```
10 READ K
20 IF K<=5 THEN 50
30 LET P = 2*(K-5)
40 GOTO 60
50 LET P = 0
60 PRINT P
70 DATA 7
80 END
```

Exercise 3, question 3

```
10 READ C,V
20 IF V<0.6*C THEN 50
30 PRINT "NOT AT 50 MI/H"
40 GOTO 70
50 PRINT "50 MI/H ALLOWED"
60 DATA 900,600
70 END
```

Teachers' Book 3a

Exercise 1

```
10 READ F,L
20 LET M = L-F
30 IF M>200 THEN 60
40 LET C = M*6
50 GOTO 70
60 LET C = 1200+1.3*(M-200)
70 PRINT C
80 DATA 4523,5223
90 END
```

Exercise 2

```
10 READ A,B,C
20 LET D = B*B-4*A*C
30 IF D<0 THEN 70
40 LET D = SQR(D)
50 PRINT D
60 GOTO 90
70 PRINT "NEGATIVE VALUE"
80 DATA 5,3,2
90 END
```

Exercise 3

```
10 READ M
20 LET C = M*2.5
30 IF C>2000 THEN 50
40 LET C = 2000
50 PRINT "NO OF COPIES =";M
60 PRINT "COST =":C
70 DATA 78
80 END
```

Exercise 4

```
10 READ C,D
20 IF C<1300 THEN 50
30 LET E = 4.5*D
40 GOTO 60
50 LET E = 4*D
60 PRINT "EXPENSES =";E;
65 PRINT " PENCE"
70 DATA 1295,73
80 END
```

Chapter 8

Book 3a

Exercise 1, question 1

```
10 READ L,W,H
20 IF L=0 THEN 70
30 LET V = L*W*H
40 PRINT V
50 GOTO 10
60 DATA 3,2,1,6.1,4.2,2.3,0,0,0
70 END
```

Exercise 1, question 2

Replace lines 10-20 as shown below:

```
10 READ H
15 IF H<0 THEN 70
20 READ M
```

Exercise 2

```
10 LET S = 0
20 READ A
30 IF A<0 THEN 60
40 LET S = S+A
50 GOTO 20
60 PRINT S
70 DATA 3.1,2.4,3.3,-1
80 END
```

Exercise 3, question 1

(a) Replace lines 30 and 40 with

```
30 IF A<78 THEN 100
40 IF A>150 THEN 100
```

(b) If we test the number of years of the person we write

```
30 IF Y<6 THEN 100
40 IF Y>12 THEN 100
```

but an extra piece of program is required to deal with the case of a person who is exactly 12 years old, since this age is included in the range. The program continues:

```
50 IF Y=12 THEN 80
60 PRINT Y,M
70 GOTO 120
80 IF M=0 THEN 60
100 PRINT "OUT OF RANGE"
110 DATA 12,0
120 END
```

Exercise 3, question 2

Insert lines 105 and 15:

```
105 GOTO 10
15 IF Y<0 THEN 120
```

Replace line 60 with

```
60 GOTO 10
```

The program ends when two negative values are read.

Exercise 4, question 1

```
10 LET N = 0
20 LET T = 0
30 READ A
40 IF A=-1 THEN 80
50 LET T = T+A
60 LET N = N+1
70 GOTO 30
80 LET M = T/N
90 PRINT M
100 DATA 93.20,111.50,84.30,-1
110 END
```

Exercise 4, question 2

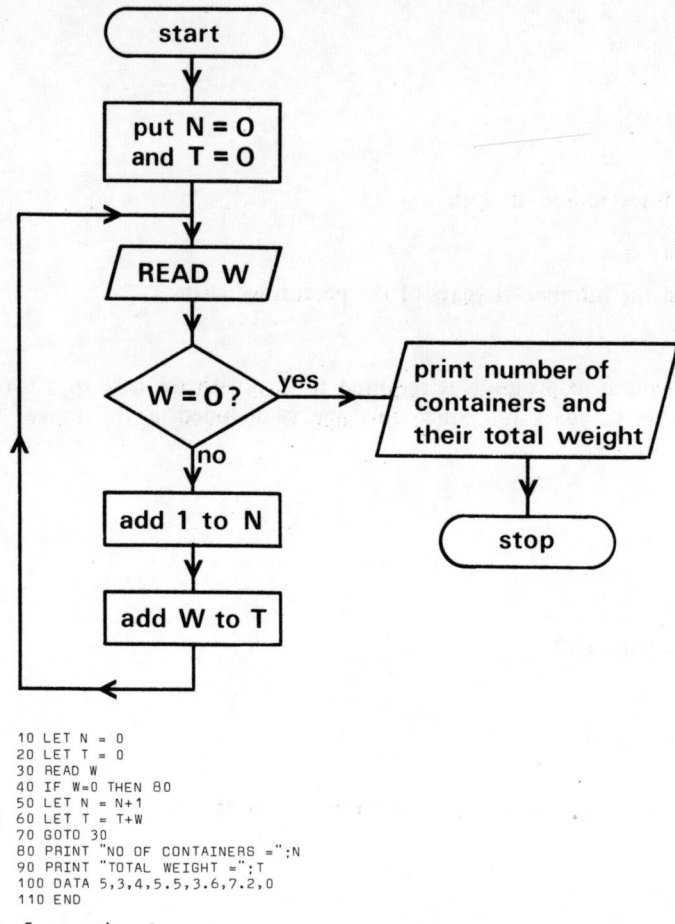

```
10 LET N = 0
20 LET T = 0
30 READ W
40 IF W=0 THEN 80
50 LET N = N+1
60 LET T = T+W
70 GOTO 30
80 PRINT "NO OF CONTAINERS =";N
90 PRINT "TOTAL WEIGHT =";T
100 DATA 5,3,4,5.5,3.6,7.2,0
110 END
```

Exercise 5, question 1

```
10 LET N = 0
20 FOR I = 1 TO 25
30 READ A
40 IF A<=10 THEN 60
50 LET N = N+1
60 NEXT I
70 PRINT N
80 DATA 5,4,11,12,9,15,17,8
90 DATA 3,23,16,4,3,15,12,7
100 DATA 2,3,4,8,16,15,2,1,2
110 END
```

Exercise 5, question 2

```
10 LET T = 0
20 FOR I = 1 TO 100
30 READ G
40 IF G<6 THEN 60
50 LET T = T+G
60 NEXT I
70 PRINT "NO OF GALLONS =";T
80 DATA 4,4,6,2,3,4,7,8,2,6
   . . . . . . . . . . .
100 END
```

Exercise 5, question 3

```
10 LET N = 0
20 FOR I = 1 TO 1000
30 READ P1,P2
40 IF P1-P2>=500 THEN 60
50 LET N = N+1
60 NEXT I
70 PRINT "NO OF CUSTOMERS";
80 PRINT " USING < 500 UNITS =";N
90 DATA 45312,44611,5031,4723
    .  .  .  .  .  .  .  .  .  .
500 END
```

Exercise 6, question 1

```
100 PRINT "DATA ERROR, ITEM";I
```

Exercise 6, question 2

```
10 LET L = 0
20 FOR I = 1 TO 1000
30 READ D
40 LET L = L+D
50 IF L>1000 THEN 70
60 NEXT I
70 PRINT "NO OF CONTRIBUTORS =";I
80 DATA 5,500,100,10,250,100,50,5
90 END
```

Notice that with the data given in the solution the first seven contributors subscribe over £1000 and the final value of £5 is not read by the program.

Exercise 6, question 3

```
10 LET W = 0
20 FOR I = 1 TO 2000
30 READ W
40 LET T = T+W
50 IF T>2000 THEN 70
60 NEXT I
70 PRINT "NO OF CONTAINERS =";I
80 DATA 15,20,18,36,14,15,23
    .  .  .  .  .  .  .  .  .  .
200 END
```

Exercise 7

```
10 FOR X = 1 TO 3 STEP 0.1
20 PRINT X,SQR(X)
30 NEXT X
40 END
```

Exercise 8, question 1

Add line 5 and change line 10:

```
5 READ N
10 FOR B = 1 TO N
```

Exercise 8, question 2

Line 5 is now changed to

```
5 READ N,M
```

and lines 10 and 30 become:

```
10 FOR B = 1 TO N
30 FOR I = 1 TO M
```

Exercise 1

```
10 LET T = 0
20 LET V = 0
30 READ C,G
40 IF C<0 THEN 90
50 LET T = T+G
60 IF C<=200 THEN 30
70 LET V = V+0.1*G
80 GOTO 30
90 PRINT "TOTAL COST =";T
100 PRINT "VAT CHARGED =";V
110 DATA 201,12,223,2,213,6,334,678,-1,-1
120 END
```

Exercise 2

```
10 READ H,M
20 IF H<12 THEN 60
25 IF H=12 THEN 40
30 LET H = H-12
40 PRINT H;".";M;" P.M."
50 GOTO 100
60 IF H<>0 THEN 80
70 LET H = 12
80 PRINT H;".";M;" A.M."
90 DATA 3,33
100 END
```

Exercise 3

```
10 READ M
20 IF M>100 THEN 50
30 PRINT "COST = £";(M*3.3)/100
40 GOTO 200
50 IF M>400 THEN 90
60 LET M = M-100
70 PRINT "COST = £";(M*1.5+330)/100
80 GOTO 200
90 LET M = M-400
100 PRINT "COST = £";(M*0.9+780)/100
110 DATA 5000
200 END
```

Exercise 4

```
10 LET A = 0
20 LET B = 0
30 LET C = 0
40 LET D = 0
50 READ X
60 IF X<0 THEN 180
70 IF X>10 THEN 100
80 LET A = A+1
90 GOTO 50
100 IF X>20 THEN 130
110 LET B = B+1
120 GOTO 50
130 IF X>30 THEN 160
140 LET C = C+1
150 GOTO 50
160 LET D = D+1
170 GOTO 50
180 PRINT "SUBJECTS IN RANGE  1-10 =";A
190 PRINT "SUBJECTS IN RANGE 11-20 =";B
200 PRINT "SUBJECTS IN RANGE 21-30 =";C
210 PRINT "SUBJECTS IN RANGE 31-40 =";D
220 DATA 17,23,32,31,23,1,32,33,21,11,12,13
230 DATA 23,25,17,18,39,1,16,37,38,23,24,12
240 DATA 13,2,5,34,6,23,14,23,31,17,27,34
250 DATA 34,24,-1,-1
260 END
```

An alternative solution to this problem uses lists. This is obviously most advantageous when a large number of categories is being counted. The alternative solution is as follows.

```
10 DIM A(4)
20 FOR I = 1 TO 4
30 LET A(I) = 0
40 NEXT I
50 READ X
60 IF X<0 THEN 100
70 LET W = INT(X/10)+1
80 LET A(W) = A(W)+1
90 GOTO 50
100 FOR I = 1 TO 4
110 LET J = 10*I
120 PRINT "SUBJECTS IN RANGE";
121 PRINT J-9;"-":J;" =";A(I)
130 NEXT I
220 DATA 17,23,32,31,23,1,32,33,21,11,12,13
230 DATA 23,25,17,18,39,1,16,37,38,23,24,12
240 DATA 13,2,5,34,6,23,14,23,31,17,27,34
250 DATA 34,24,-1,-1
260 END
```

Exercise 5

```
10 LET T = 0
20 PRINT "PLAYED","GOALS","AVERAGE"
30 PRINT
40 FOR I = 1 TO 30
50 READ G
60 LET T = T+G
70 PRINT I,T,T/I
80 NEXT I
90 DATA 1,3,2,3,0,0,2,1,3,2,5,0,0,0,0
91 DATA 2,0,1,1,1,2,3,0,1,0,7,0,1,2
100 END
```

Exercise 6

```
10 LET S = 0
20 LET N = 0
30 LET T = 0
40 FOR I = 1 TO 28
50 READ C,M
60 LET S = S+M
70 IF M<=T THEN 100
80 LET N = C
90 LET T = M
100 IF M<80 THEN 120
110 PRINT C,M
120 NEXT I
130 PRINT "AVERAGE MARK =";S/28
140 PRINT "WINNER IS CANDIDATE NO";N;
141 PRINT " WITH";T;" MARKS"
150 DATA 10,81,13,72,44,83,64,75,143,67,33,86
151 DATA 127,68,44,85,93,51,76,71,203,86,217,93
152 DATA 48,75,53,81,147,56,121,68,153,74
153 DATA 163,85,72,66,9,57,28,75,83,47,99,85
154 DATA 146,73,152,86,161,86,211,63,58,80
160 END
```

Exercise 7

```
10 LET S = 0
20 FOR I = 1 TO 100
30 LET S = S+I*I
40 IF S>1000 THEN 60
50 NEXT I
60 PRINT "TOTAL =";S,"NO OF TERMS =";I
70 END
```

Exercise 8

```
10 PRINT "SPEED,KM/H",
11 PRINT "STOPPING DISTANCE,METRES"
20 FOR V = 10 TO 150 STEP 10
30 PRINT V,0.2*V+0.006*V*V
40 NEXT V
50 END
```

Exercise 9

```
10 PRINT "NUMBER","SQUARE","CUBE"
20 FOR X = 1 TO 4.05 STEP 0.1
30 LET W = X*X
40 PRINT X,W,X*W
50 NEXT X
60 END
```

Notice the end value of 4·05 in the loop to ensure that the last value is printed.

Exercise 10

Replace the constants in line 20 by A, B+ 0·5*H, and H. Insert a statement to read A, B and H.

Chapter 9

Book 3a

Exercise 1, question 1

```
10 DIM A(20)
20 FOR I = 1 TO 20
30 READ A(I)
40 NEXT I
50 LET W = A(1)
60 FOR I = 2 TO 20
70 IF W<=A(I) THEN 90
80 LET W = A(I)
90 NEXT I
100 PRINT "SMALLEST NUMBER =";W
110 DATA 7,3,6,8,9,5,2,3,4,9
120 DATA 8,3,7,5,6,5,4,3,4,8
130 END
```

Exercise 1, question 2

```
10 DIM N(20)
20 FOR I = 1 TO 20
30 READ N(I)
40 NEXT I
50 LET M = N(1)
60 LET P = 1
70 FOR I = 2 TO 20
80 IF M<=N(I) THEN 110
90 LET M = N(I)
100 LET P = I
110 NEXT I
120 PRINT M,P
130 DATA 7,3,6,8,9,5,2,3,4,9
140 DATA 8,3,7,5,6,5,4,3,4,8
150 END
```

Exercise 1, question 3

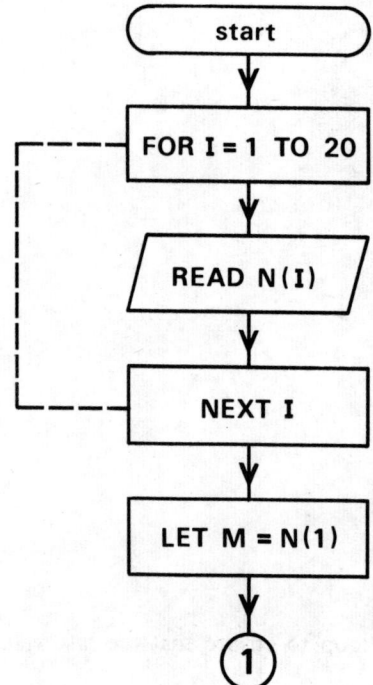

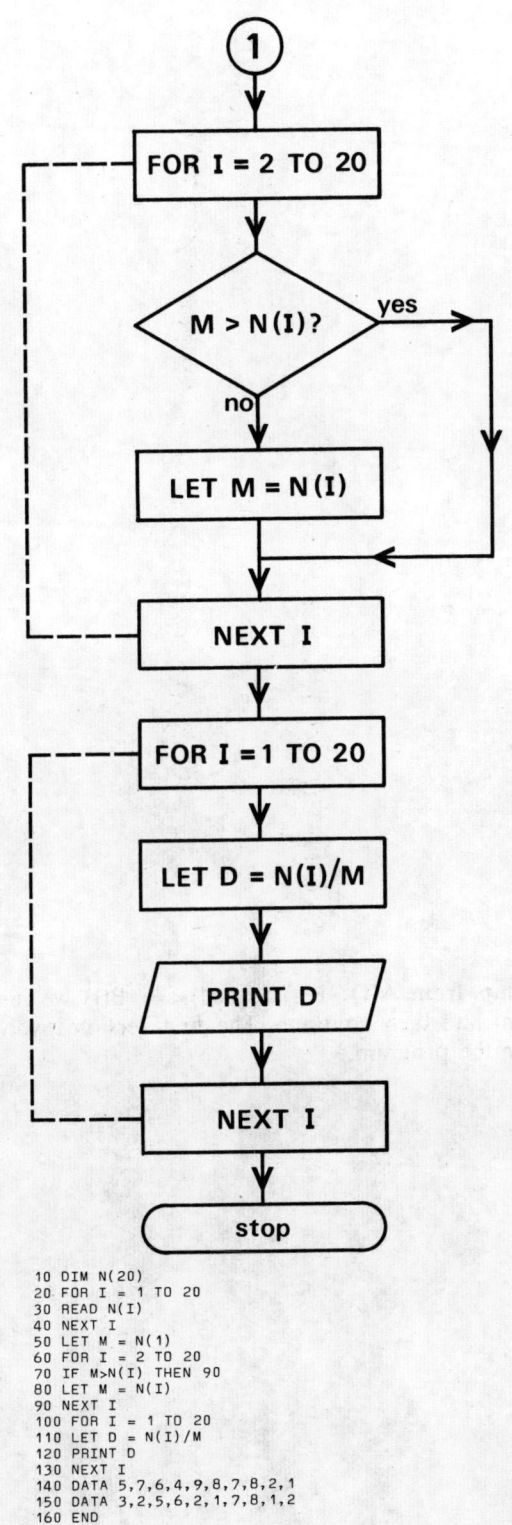

```
10 DIM N(20)
20 FOR I = 1 TO 20
30 READ N(I)
40 NEXT I
50 LET M = N(1)
60 FOR I = 2 TO 20
70 IF M>N(I) THEN 90
80 LET M = N(I)
90 NEXT I
100 FOR I = 1 TO 20
110 LET D = N(I)/M
120 PRINT D
130 NEXT I
140 DATA 5,7,6,4,9,8,7,8,2,1
150 DATA 3,2,5,6,2,1,7,8,1,2
160 END
```

Exercise 1, question 4

```
10 DIM D(7)
20 LET S = 0
30 FOR I = 1 TO 7
40 READ D(I)
50 LET S = S+D(I)
60 NEXT I
70 LET C = 100/S
80 FOR I = 1 TO 7
90 PRINT D(I)*C
100 NEXT I
110 DATA 17,14,25,13,16,25,31
120 END
```

Exercise 1, question 5

```
10 DIM T(25)
20 FOR I = 1 TO 25
30 READ T(I)
40 NEXT I
50 LET A1 = 0
60 LET A2 = 0
70 LET A3 = 0
80 FOR I = 1 TO 25
90 LET A1 = A1+T(I)
100 NEXT I
110 FOR I = 1 TO 10
120 LET A2 = A2+T(I)
130 NEXT I
140 FOR I = 16 TO 25
150 LET A3 = A3+T(I)
160 NEXT I
170 PRINT "OVERALL AVERAGE =";A1/25
180 PRINT "AV. OVER 1ST TEN =";A2/10
190 PRINT "AV. OVER LAST TEN =";A3/10
200 DATA 10.32,10.34,10.31,10.30,10.34
    . . . . . . . . . . . . . . . .
250 END
```

Exercise 2, question 1

```
10 DIM A(12),B(12)
20 FOR I = 1 TO 12
30 READ A(I)
40 NEXT I
50 FOR I = 1 TO 12
60 READ B(I)
70 NEXT I
80 FOR I = 1 TO 12
90 IF B(I)<A(I)+20 THEN 110
100 PRINT I,B(I)
110 NEXT I
120 DATA 43,18,40,71,93,110
    . . . . . . . . . .
150 END
```

Exercise 2, question 2

By changing the relationship from $A(I) > B(I)$ to $A(I) <= B(I)$ we jump round the PRINT statement and then continue. The first version involves an extra jump instruction in the program.

Exercise 2, question 3

```
10 DIM A(12),B(12),C(12)
20 FOR I = 1 TO 12
30 READ A(I)
40 NEXT I
50 FOR I = 1 TO 12
60 READ B(I)
70 NEXT I
80 FOR I =1 TO 12
90 LET C(I) = A(I)+B(I)
100 NEXT I
110 LET M = C(1)
120 FOR I = 1 TO 12
130 IF M>C(I) THEN 150
140 LET M = C(I)
150 NEXT I
160 PRINT "LARGEST SALE =";M
170 DATA 43,18,40,71,93,110
    . . . . . . . . . .
200 END
```

Exercise 3

(i) ```10 DIM(40,5)```

(ii) ```20 DIM(50,3)```

Exercise 4

$A(1,1) = 2, A(1,2) = 1, A(1,3) = 1$
$A(2,1) = 4, A(2,2) = 3, A(2,3) = 5$

Teachers' Book 3a

Exercise 1

```
10 DIM A(40)
20 LET S = 0
30 FOR I = 1 TO 40
40 READ A(I)
50 LET S = S+A(I)
60 NEXT I
70 LET S = S/40
80 LET C = 0
90 FOR I = 1 TO 40
100 IF A(I)<=2*S THEN 130
110 PRINT A(I)
120 LET C = C+1
130 NEXT I
140 IF C>0 THEN 220
150 PRINT "NO VALUES GREATER THAN";
160 PRINT " TWICE THE MEAN"
170 REM IF A VALUE>2S HAS BEEN FOUND
180 REM C>0 AND THE.MESSAGE IS NOT OUTPUT
190 DATA 5,6,3,-1,4,8,10,-3,7,10,2,-7,-8
200 DATA 4,1,6,5,2,-8,3,-4,2,1,2,3,2,1
210 DATA 2,3,12,1,3,18,-6,-20,1,1,2,1,0
220 END
```

Exercise 2

```
10 DIM A(20),B(20),C(20)
20 FOR I = 1 TO 20
30 READ A(I)
40 LET B(I) = A(I)*A(I)
50 LET C(I) = B(I)-A(I)
60 NEXT I
70 LET S1 = 0
80 LET S2 = 0
90 LET S3 = 0
100 FOR I = 1 TO 20
110 LET S1 = S1+A(I)
120 LET S2 = S2+B(I)
130 LET S3 = S3+C(I)
140 NEXT I
150 PRINT S1,S2,S3
160 DATA 1,2,4,3,6,5,8,4,3,2
170 DATA 2,3,1,4,3,4,6,5,8,6
180 END
```

Exercise 3

```
10 LET S1 = 0
20 LET S2 = 0
30 FOR I = 1 TO 20
40 READ M
50 LET S1 = S1+M
60 LET S2 = S2+M*M
70 NEXT I
80 PRINT S1,S2,S2-S1
160 DATA 1,2,4,3,6,5,8,4,3,2
170 DATA 2,3,1,4,3,4,6,5,8,6
180 END
```

Exercise 4

```
10 DIM N(50)
20 FOR I = 1 TO 50
30 READ N(I)
40 NEXT I
50 FOR I = 1 TO 50
60 IF N(I)>=0 THEN 80
70 PRINT I
80 NEXT I
110 DATA 5,3,-1,-2,4,8,3,2,1,-1,-6,-3,-2
120 DATA 2,3,1,-4,-5,-2,1,2,3,1,4,5,1,9
130 DATA 3,-4,-5,1,2,3,4,2,1,3,-3,-4,-8
140 DATA 3,-2,-2,-4,1,-3,-4,-3,-4,-1
150 END
```

Exercise 5

```
10 DIM A(50)
20 FOR I = 1 TO 50
30 READ W
40 IF W>=0 THEN 60
50 LET W = -W
60 LET A(I) = W
70 NEXT I
80 FOR I = 1 TO 50
90 PRINT SQR(A(I))
100 NEXT I
110 DATA 5,3,-1,-2,4,8,3,2,1,-1,-6,-3,-2
120 DATA 2,3,1,-4,-5,-2,1,2,3,1,4,5,1,9
130 DATA 3,-4,-5,1,2,3,4,2,1,3,-3,-4,-8
140 DATA 3,-2,-2,-4,1,-3,-4,-3,-4,-1
150 END
```

Exercise 6

```
10 DIM T(8),A(8)
20 LET S1 = 0
30 LET S2 = 0
40 FOR I = 1 TO 8
50 READ T(I)
60 LET S1 = S1+T(I)
70 NEXT I
80 FOR I = 1 TO 8
90 READ A(I)
100 LET S2 = S2+A(I)
110 NEXT I
120 LET H = 0
130 LET L = 100
140 FOR I = 1 TO 8
150 IF T(I)<=H THEN 170.
160 LET H = T(I)
170 IF T(I)>L THEN 190
180 LET L = T(I)
190 NEXT I
200 LET S1 = (S1-H-L)/6
210 LET H = 0
220 LET L = 100
230 FOR I = 1 TO 8
240 IF A(I)<=H THEN 260
250 LET H = A(I)
260 IF A(I)>L THEN 280
270 LET L = A(I)
280 NEXT I
290 LET S2 = (S2-H-L)/6
300 PRINT "MARK FOR TECHNIQUE =";S1
310 PRINT "MARK FOR ARTISTRY =";S2
320 DATA 5.6,5.8,5.7,5.7,5.4,5.6,5.8,5.7
330 DATA 5.4,5.7,5.7,5.8,5.4,5.3,5.4,5.6
340 END
```

Exercise 7

```
10 DIM A(8),B(8)
20 FOR I = 1 TO 8
30 READ A(I)
40 NEXT I
50 READ N
60 IF N<0 THEN 230
70 FOR I = 1 TO 8
80 READ B(I)
90 NEXT I
100 FOR I = 1 TO 8
110 IF A(I)=B(I) THEN 130
120 GOTO 50
130 NEXT I
140 PRINT "COMPETITOR NO.":N
150 GOTO 50
160 DATA 4,1,8,7,5,2,6,3
170 DATA 27,4,3,1,2,7,6,8,5
180 DATA 36,5,3,2,1,4,8,6,7
190 DATA 44,4,1,8,7,5,2,3,6
200 DATA 45,4,1,8,7,5,2,6,3
210 DATA 49,1,2,3,4,5,6,7,8
220 DATA -1
230 END
```

Exercise 8

```
10 DIM R(40,5),H(5)
20 READ N
30 FOR I = 1 TO N
40 FOR J = 1 TO 5
50 READ R(I,J)
60 NEXT J
70 NEXT I
80 FOR I = 1 TO 5
90 LET M = 0
100 FOR J = 1 TO N
110 IF R(J,I)<M THEN 130
120 LET M = R(J,I)
130 NEXT J
140 LET H(I) = M
150 NEXT I
160 PRINT "HIGHEST MARKS"
170 FOR I = 1 TO 5
180 PRINT "SUBJECT";I;" =";H(I)
190 NEXT I
200 DATA 7
210 DATA 38,49,51,43,39
220 DATA 47,58,61,46,49
230 DATA 58,53,73,52,56
240 DATA 46,51,72,43,52
250 DATA 60,57,71,49,55
260 DATA 54,55,69,55,52
270 DATA 35,47,61,48,53
280 END
```

Exercise 9

```
10 DIM Q(20,4)
20 FOR I = 1 TO 20
30 FOR J = 1 TO 4
40 READ Q(I,J)
50 NEXT J
60 NEXT I
70 FOR I = 1 TO 4
80 LET S = 0
90 FOR J = 1 TO 20
100 IF Q(J,I)<3 THEN 120
110 LET S = S+1
120 NEXT J
130 PRINT "PROPERTY";I;":";
140 PRINT S;" MARKS OF THREE OR MORE"
150 NEXT I
155 PRINT
156 PRINT
160 FOR I = 1 TO 4
170 LET S = 0
180 FOR J = 1 TO 20
190 LET S = S+Q(J,I)
200 NEXT J
210 PRINT "PROPERTY";I;":";
220 PRINT " AVERAGE MARK SCORED:";S/20
230 NEXT I
235 PRINT
236 PRINT
240 LET S = 0
250 FOR I = 1 TO 20
260 FOR J = 1 TO 4
270 IF Q(I,J)<=3 THEN 300
280 NEXT J
290 LET S = S+1
300 NEXT I
310 PRINT "NO. GIVING MORE THAN THREE "
311 PRINT "MARKS TO EACH PROPERTY:";S
312 PRINT
313 PRINT
320 LET S = 0
330 FOR I = 1 TO 20
340 FOR J = 1 TO 4
350 IF Q(I,J)=1 THEN 380
360 NEXT J
370 GOTO 390
380 LET S = S+1
390 NEXT I
400 PRINT "NO. GIVING A MARK OF ONE =";S
405 LET S = 0
410 FOR I = 1 TU 20
420 IF Q(I,1)<=2 THEN 450
430 IF Q(I,4)>2 THEN 450
440 LET S = S+1
450 NEXT I
455 PRINT
456 PRINT
460 PRINT "NO. GIVING OVER 2 MARKS TO PROP. 1";
461 PRINT " AND LESS THAN 3 TO PROP. 4 =";S
500 DATA 5,3,4,1,4,2,3,1,2,3,3,4,3,4,3,4
501 DATA 3,4,4,4,1,1,2,3,1,3,5,5,4,4,4,4
502 DATA 3,4,5,5,1,2,1,2,4,3,5,5,5,4,3,2
503 DATA 3,4,5,1,4,1,2,3,5,4,5,4,5,2,4,2
504 DATA 1,4,5,5,4,4,1,2,5,1,4,2,1,3,3,4
510 END
```

Chapter 10

No exercises in Book 3a

Exercise 1

```
1 GOTO 26
2 PRINT "JAN    ":
3 GOTO 110
4 PRINT "FEB    ":
5 GOTO 110
6 PRINT "MAR    ":
7 GOTO 110
8 PRINT "APR    ":
9 GOTO 110
10 PRINT "MAY    ":
11 GOTO 110
12 PRINT "JUN    ":
13 GOTO 110
14 PRINT "JUL    ":
15 GOTO 110
16 PRINT "AUG    ":
17 GOTO 110
18 PRINT "SEP    ":
19 GOTO 110
20 PRINT "OCT    ":
21 GOTO 110
22 PRINT "NOV    ":
23 GOTO 110
24 PRINT "DEC    ":
25 GOTO110
26 DIM M(12)
27 FOR I = 1 TO 12
30 LET M(I) = 0
40 NEXT I
50 READ A
60 IF A<0 THEN 90
70 LET M(A) = M(A)+1
80 GOTO 50
90 FOR A = 1 TO 12
100 PRINT
101 ON A GOTO 2,4,6,8,10,12,14,16,18,20,22,24
110 FOR I = 1 TO M(A)
120 PRINT "*";
130 NEXT I
140 NEXT A
150 PRINT
160 PRINT
170 PRINT "HISTOGRAM OF NUMBERS OF BIRTHDAYS"
180 PRINT "PER MONTH IN A SAMPLE POPULATION"
190 GOTO 250
245 DATA 1,2,3,4,5,6,7,8,9,1,3,5,7,9,2,4,6,8
246 DATA 10,10,10,10,10,3,3,3,3,3,3,3,3,3,4
247 DATA 4,4,5,5,5,5,6,6,6,11,11,11,11,12,12
248 DATA 12,12,11,3,5,4,7,7,7,8,8,8,9,10,-1
250 END
```

Exercise 2

```
10 FOR I = 1 TO 7
20 PRINT TAB(7+I);12+111*I
30 NEXT I
40 END
```

Exercise 3

```
10 DEF FNP(A) = INT(100*A+0.5)/100
20 READ A
25 IF A<0 THEN- 200
30 PRINT "CLASS 1 CUSTOMER"
40 PRINT "COST =";FNP(1.1*A)
50 PRINT
60 PRINT "CLASS 2 CUSTOMER"
70 PRINT "COST =";FNP(1.1*A)
80 PRINT "WITH DISCOUNT";FNP(1.05*A)
90 PRINT "WITH DISCOUNT AND"
100 PRINT "DUTY RECOVERED";FNP(1.02*A)
105 GOTO 20
110 DATA 100,25.25,4332,-1
200 END
```

Exercise 4

```
10 GOSUB 1000
20 READ A,B,C,D,E,F,G
30 PRINT A,B,C,D,E,F,G
40 GOSUB 1000
50 PRINT "THE COMPUTER"
60 PRINT "YOURS OBEDIENTLY"
70 GOSUB 1000
80 LET X = 100
90 LET Y = 200
100 PRINT "ANSWER IS",X
110 GOSUB 1000
120 PRINT "A =",X,"B =",Y
130 GOSUB 1000
140 PRINT A,B,C,D,E,F,G
150 PRINT "ANSWER IS",X
160 PRINT "A =",X,"B =",Y
170 GOSUB 1000
180 PRINT "A = ";X,"B = ";Y
190 GOSUB 1000
200 LET A = 5
210 PRINT "A = ";A,
220 LET B = A*100
230 PRINT "B = ";B
240 GOSUB 1000
250 PRINT "A = ";A
260 PRINT "B = ";B
270 GOSUB 1000
280 GOTO 1040
500 DATA 50,51,52,53,54,55,56
1000 FOR I = 1 TO 10
1010 PRINT
1020 NEXT I
1030 RETURN
1040 END
```

Exercise 5

Insert a GOSUB statement at line 45 and then write the twenty new statements as a subroutine at the end of the program. (The same effect can be obtained by using an ordinary GOTO statement and finishing the twenty statements with GOTO 50.)

Chapter 11

No exercises in Book 3a

Teachers' Book 3a

Exercise 1

Insert the line

```
605 IF V = 6 THEN 640
```

Exercise 2

Insert the following lines:

```
191 IF P1<>0 THEN 200
192 GOSUB 500
193 IF V=6 THEN 200
194 GOTO 320

321 IF P2<>0 THEN 330
322 GOSUB 500
323 IF V=6 THEN 330
324 GOTO 190
```

Note that at line 191 a test is made to see if Player 1 has started. If he has (i.e. if P1 is not zero), a jump is made to line 200, where the die is thrown and its value is added to his current position. If he has not started, the die is thrown instead in line 192. If he now throws a six he goes to line 200, otherwise play passes to his opponent by the jump to line 320. A similar argument applies for Player 2 in lines 321-324.

Exercise 3

Insert the following lines:

```
265 IF P1<>P2 THEN 270
266 LET P1 = P1-V
267 PRINT "SAME SQUARE AS NO 2, ";
268 PRINT "GO BACK TO SQUARE ";P1

395 IF P2<>P1 THEN 400
396 LET P2 = P2-V
397 PRINT "SAME SQUARE AS NO 1, ";
398 PRINT "GO BACK TO SQUARE ";P1
```